D1189853

AFC BOURNEMOUTH
Miscellany

AFC BOURNEMOUTH
Miscellany

Cherries Trivia,
History, Facts & Stats

TONY MATTHEWS

AFC BOURNEMOUTH
Miscellany

Cherries Trivia,
History, Facts & Stats

All statistics, facts and figures are correct as of 1st August 2015

© Tony Matthews

Tony Matthews has asserted his rights in accordance with the Copyright, Designs and Patents Act 1988 to be identified as the author of this work.

Published By:
Pitch Publishing (Brighton) Ltd
A2 Yeoman Gate
Yeoman Way
Durrington
BN13 3QZ

Email: info@pitchpublishing.co.uk
Web: www.pitchpublishing.co.uk

Published 2015

A catalogue record for this book is available from the British Library

ISBN 9781785310829

Typesetting and origination by Pitch Publishing
Printed in India by Replika Press Pvt. Ltd.

DEDICATION

This book is dedicated to all the players who, over the last 116 years, have represented AFC Bournemouth through thick and thin, especially those under influential manager Eddie Howe, who starred for the Club in the hugely successful 2014/15 season when Premier League and top-flight football came to the Club for the first time.

ACKNOWLEDGMENTS

I would like to say a special thank you to Paul at Pitch Publishing for agreeing to produce and publish this book, my 135th on football (1975 to date), but my first on AFC Bournemouth… and what a great time to do it!

Also, I have to thank Max Fitzgerald, head of media and communications at the Club; Vince Bartram, a former Cherries goalkeeper and a good friend of mine from yesteryear; Derek Hammond (Pitch Publishing); ardent supporters Steven Matthews (my nephew from Bo'ness, Scotland), Geoff Bentham, Tim Carroll, Bill Greenaway, Graham Jones, Vic Kenning, Sid Martin, Stuart McPherson, Leslie Oakham and Frank Peters; fans of other clubs, namely Geoff Faraday, Robert Stone, Michael Setterfield, Jonathan Harris, Nick Lange, Gordon Thomas and Bob Martin; top photographer Malcolm Armstrong and last, but by no means least, a special thank you, as always, to my loving, and indeed, long-suffering yet understanding wife Margaret, who once again has had to withstand the noise of my fingers tapping away on the computer keyboard, seeing scores of programmes, magazines, newspapers and reference books scattered all over the floor, as well as listening to me moaning and groaning, especially when the computer crashes, things go wrong or I can't match up the figures and stats!

FOREWORD

Although AFC Bournemouth has only been a member of the Football League since 1923, there are 1,001 things many supporters, and certainly players, simply do not know about the Cherries! That will change when you read through these pages of this excellent book put together by Tony M, an old friend of mine from my days in the Midlands. He has picked out of the hat, and found in the archives, scores of interesting and quite fascinating facts and figures, stories and statistics, which will certainly get fans, wherever they are – in pubs, clubs, houses, on board coaches and trains, and in cars travelling to away games, even sitting in the stands watching a game – talking and arguing, about past events and ex-players. And even the neutral supporter, the football lovers in general, will enjoy this mini-encyclopaedia. As a footballer you are paid to go out and try to become part of the club's history. I am proud to have done that, having been associated with the Cherries for over 20 years. I knew a little about the Club's history before I was signed but, prior to reading this book, if you asked me a question about something from the past, I would struggle to come up with a definitive answer. Now I certainly know a lot more than I did. And you will too once you have digested what's on the pages that follow. And what a great time to read and enjoy following the Cherries' promotion to the Premier League, rising into the top flight of League football for the very first time in the Club's history.

Vince Bartram

* Vince made 361 league appearances during his career (132 for the Cherries: 1991–94). He is now a goalkeeping coach with Southampton.

It was a great privilege to be asked to write this foreword. Bournemouth is a family club, a great club, which is now going through one of the finest periods in its history. A local lad, born in Poole, I was an avid Bournemouth fan and I had the privilege of spending ten very enjoyable years as a player at Dean Court, serving under two fine managers, Harry Redknapp and Tony Pulis. As a team, we had several exciting moments with cup runs, promotion challenges and relegation battles, and this book brings back many fond memories, especially the 1984 Associate Members Cup Final when I had the pleasure of scoring the winning goal against Hull City. The 1950s – a golden era of the Club – is featured in depth in this excellent book which is jam-packed full with stats and facts, some I never knew about! Reading about those epic FA Cup triumphs over some previous winners of the trophy, Manchester United, Tottenham Hotspur and Wolves, will certainly revive memories for he older supporters, and then we had some great seasons in the 1980s and now everything is buzzing with Premier League football coming to Bournemouth – a thing truthfully I never thought would happen! Eddie Howe has done a terrific job and everyone now is looking forward to a new era at The Goldsands Stadium (now named the Vitality Stadium). But first sit down and read this book – it's fascinating. You'll be amazed what has happened at AFC Bournemouth over the last 116 years.

Paul Morrell

* Paul appeared in almost 380 games for the Cherries (343 in the league) between 1983 and 1993. He now works for the National Probation Service in Bournemouth.

AFC Bournemouth Miscellany

A BRIEF HISTORY OF AFC BOURNEMOUTH

From the day Bournemouth were first formed, towards the end of the 19th century, headlines have been made, some for good reasons, some for bad. It is said that the Club was formed in the autumn of 1899. Rising out of the remains of Boscombe St. John's Lads' Institute FC, it was called Boscombe FC and its first president was Mr J.C. Nutt. In its first season, that of 1899/1900, the Club competed in the local Bournemouth and District Junior League, and also entered the Hampshire Junior Cup. For two years the team occupied a pitch in Castlemain Avenue, Pokesdown but, in the early 1900s, the home venue was switched to King's Park. After making good progress – one game resulted in a 12-0 win – in 1905/06 Boscombe FC graduated to senior amateur football and did very well, so much so that in the summer of 1910 the Club was granted a long term lease on a strip of wasteland next to Kings Park, courtesy of the then–president, Mr. J.E. Cooper-Dean. Now technically 'owning' a ground, the club's officials chose to name it Dean Court after the benefactor and, as the team continued to thrive on the field, dominating the local football scene, the first professional player was signed, Harry Baven Penton. Around this time, Boscombe FC adopted their present-day nickname 'The Cherries', chosen perhaps from their Dean Court ground which, at the time, was surrounded by a vast cherry orchard!

INTO THE FA CUP

The Cherries participated in the FA Cup for the first time in 1913/14, but the following year the club's progress was halted by the outbreak of the First World War, at which point Boscombe FC returned to the Hampshire League. In 1920, the Third Division was formed and with club's moving up from the Southern League, this paved the way for Boscombe FC to enter a higher class of football. In 1923, the Club changed its name to Bournemouth and Boscombe Athletic FC, and during this year membership was gained to the Third Division South of the Football League. The Cherries' first match, away to Swindon Town in August 1923, ended in a 3-1 defeat, but soon afterwards, the first home League game took place at Dean Court, also against Swindon, which ended 0-0 in front of 7,000 fans, thus bringing the Cherries their first league point.Bournemouth struggled early on in the Football League, but eventually they established themselves as a solid unit and went on to create a record for the longest stay in the third tier of English football, eventually leaving it in April 1970 when they slipped into the Fourth Division. Bournemouth had to wait until just after the Second World War before winning their first major trophy, beating Walsall in the Third Division South Cup Final at Stamford Bridge in 1946. They qualified for the semi-finals by finishing top of the South Region qualifying competition and a 1-0 replay victory over QPR took them through to the final. During the late 1940s the Cherries comfortably held their own and then, in the 50s, things really started to happen out on the pitch.

GIANTKILLERS

In 1956/57, under manager Freddie Cox, Bournemouth pulled off two superb FA Cup giantkilling acts, dumping out Wolves (away) and Tottenham Hotspur (home) before losing to double-chasing Manchester United in the quarter-finals. The team's overall play was steady throughout the 1960s, and two years after John Bond had moved in as manager (following relegation in 1970), the Club adopted the more streamlined AFC Bournemouth title. This, however, is only a trade name as the Club is still officially registered as Bournemouth and Boscombe Athletic Football Club. In 1984, the Cherries, with former player Harry Redknapp now bedded in as manager, registered another famous victory by knocking the holders Manchester United out of the FA Cup, and three years later Redknapp guided the team into the second tier of the Football League for the first time in the club's history as Third Division champions. Comfortably surviving their first season in the Second Division, the Cherries made a serious challenge for promotion to the top flight in 1988/89, but unfortunately fell away after a poor run of results late in the campaign. But their final placing of 12th remained their highest finish in the Football League until 2013/14. On the final day of the 1989/90 season, Leeds United visited Dean Court with an eye on winning the Second Division title, while Bournemouth effectively needed a result (a win or draw at least) to stay up. Unfortunately there were several skirmishes involving away fans in the town and around the ground before the start of the game and, after a tense and nervy contest, Leeds ran out 1-0 winners and went up, while Bournemouth were relegated. This was a sad day for the Cherries.

CHANGE OF MANAGERS

Redknapp remained as manager at Dean Court until 1992, his last season ending with the club missing out on the play-offs by a mere three points. However, mounting financial pressures had caused him to resign. On leaving, he rejoined his former club West Ham as first team coach under boss Billy Bonds. Redknapp's successor was former player Tony Pulis who assembled a much cheaper squad, but the team could only manage consecutive 17th place finishes before he walked out, blaming his departure on the financial state of the club at that time. Bournemouth, without a manager, made a dreadful start to the 1994/95 campaign, losing their first seven matches and 12 of their first 14. They actually picked up only ten points out of a possible 69 up to the turn of the year, and were propping up the division with one home attendance falling to just 2,505. Despite a minor upturn in form, following the arrival of boss Mel Machin, the Cherries knew they had it all to do if they were to survive – there were five teams facing relegation this term as the format of the league changed. Thankfully, an excellent late run, combined with surprise collapses on the behalf of fellow relegation rivals Cambridge United and Plymouth Argyle, saw the Cherries survive on the last day of the season by two points. They beat Shrewsbury Town 3-0 in front of an ecstatic near full-house crowd at Dean Court of 10,737. Machin, another former Bournemouth player (1970–73), remained in charge for six years, during which time the Cherries claimed several mid-table finishes. In 1998/99 the team made a serious play-off challenge but ultimately fell short again, ending up seventh before slipping down to 16th in 1999/2000. Early in the 2000/01 season, Machin was dismissed as manager, but remained with the club as director of football.

NEW GROUND

Yet another ex-player, Sean O'Driscoll, was promoted from the coaching staff to replace Machin and it took him some time to get the team back on track – they had won only two and drawn seven of their first 16 league games, banking 13 points out of a possible 48. In his first season in charge, O'Driscoll saw Bournemouth narrowly miss out on the play-offs, but sadly the Cherries were relegated a year later, having moved into their new redeveloped ground, The Goldsands Stadium. O'Driscoll stuck in there, and he and his players were rewarded with promotion via the Third Division play-offs in 2002/03 – the Cherries beating Lincoln City 5-2 in the final at the Millennium Stadium. Bournemouth narrowly missed out on the play-offs in 2003/04 (the season when James Hayter scored the fastest-ever hat-trick in league football in a 6-0 win over Wrexham) and it was another case of so near yet so far in 2004/05, while in stark contrast, the Cherries almost went down in 2005/06, before O'Driscoll eventually left, replaced by yet another former player, Kevin Bond, son of John, who had made 126 league appearances for the club between 1988 and 1992.

ADMINISTRATION WORRIES

In February 2008 Bournemouth were forced into administration, deducted ten points, slipped into the relegation zone (again) and, with debts of around £4m, almost went out of business. The off-field uncertainty continued throughout the season, at the end of which the Cherries were relegated to League 2. And prior to the 2008/09 season, the club's future in league football was again put in doubt when the authorities threatened to block Bournemouth's participation in League 2, due to problems with the team's continuing administration and change in ownership. In fact, the Cherries were asked to complete all fixtures and get out of administration. But the tough thing was that the team had to continue with a 17-point deduction, a penalty for failing to follow the regulation insolvency rules. The new company was also ordered to pay unsecured creditors the amount offered at the time of the original CVA (around ten pence in the pound) within two years. Early in 2008/09 manager Bond was sacked, replaced by yet another former player, Irishman Jimmy Quinn, who would himself leave the club after just a few months in charge. Next into the hot seat (on a caretaker basis) came ex-Bournemouth player Eddie Howe, aged 31, who took over the reins when the Cherries were still languishing at the wrong end of League 2, some ten points adrift of bottom spot. Around this time, it was announced that local businessman Adam Murry had completed the purchase of 50 per cent of the club's shares from previous chairman Paul Baker. However, in January 2009, Murry missed the deadline to buy those shares. The Cherries retained Football League status by winning their last home game of 2008/09, beating Grimsby Town 2-1 in front of 9,008 nervous fans, Steve Fletcher netting the winning goal ten minutes from time. That was certainly the 'Great Escape' and the Cherries then finished their troubled season by recording their best away win for 30 years – whipping Morecambe 4-0.

NEW ERA BEGINS

In June 2009, a consortium, including Adam Murry, took over AFC Bournemouth and, to celebrate his first full season in charge, manager Howe led the Cherries to promotion with two games remaining. However, he then surprisingly left the club for Burnley. Lee Bradbury took over and he guided the team into the League 1 play-offs in 2010/11, but the two-legged semi-final against Huddersfield Town ended in bitter disappointment as the Terriers won the penalty shootout 4-2 (following a 3-3 draw after extra time). After failing to get Bournemouth into a promotion challenging position for a second time, Bradbury was replaced by youth coach Paul Groves for the final games of 2011/12. Groves stayed in charge until October 2012 when previous boss Eddie Howe returned with the Cherries struggling at the wrong end of the table. And not only did Howe pull the club out of trouble, he guided them to promotion to the Championship and a place in the second tier of English football for the first time since 1990. Prior to the 2013/14 season, Bournemouth invited Real Madrid to the Goldsands Stadium for a friendly. A record crowd turned up to see the Spanish giants win 6-0. Despite that heavy defeat, the Cherries made a promising start to life in the Championship and eventually took tenth place, their highest-ever finish in the Football League although, on a low note, the club announced a loss of £10.3m. But things got even better out on the pitch the following season.

THE PREMIER LEAGUE BECKONS

After a very efficient start, with positive results at home and away, in October the Cherries thrashed Birmingham City 8-0 at St Andrew's – the first time the team had ever scored eight goals in a legitimate league game (a 10-0 victory over Northampton Town in September 1939 was subsequently declared null and void due to the outbreak of the Second World War). And later in the month, the Cherries knocked Premier League side West Bromwich Albion out of the League Cup to reach the quarter-finals of this competition for the first time in the club's history. They lost, however, to Liverpool at home in the next round. After that flurry of activity, the Cherries battled hard and long to stay at the top end of the Championship and after some terrific displays, they surged through, amid great excitement, to gain promotion to the Premier League – thus reaching the top flight of English football for the first time. After drawing their penultimate home league game against Sheffield Wednesday 2-2, when Simon Francis was sent off and Adam Smith conceded a stoppage-time penalty, they knew that victory in their final one against Bolton Wanderers would effectively seal a place with the elite. On a night of passion, high drama, tension and great joy, the Cherries went out and performed with style, panache and confidence, beating the Trotters 3-0 to spark off elaborate celebrations, never seen in the town before, which went on and on and on. And there's a lot more to come from Eddie Howe and his merry men as AFC Bournemouth – Dorset's only Football League club – aim to beat the best in the land.

Tony Matthews
Summer 2015

INTO THE PREMIER LEAGUE AS CHAMPIONSHIP CHAMPIONS

The diary of how AFC Bournemouth won the Football League Championship to gain promotion to the Premier League in 2014/15. After playing 11 pre-season friendlies, seven of which were won, including a 3-1 victory over Swansea City, a 3-2 win at Portsmouth, a 2-2 draw with FC Copenhagen in Austria and an 11-0 whipping of neighbours Dorchester Town, the Cherries began their journey towards the top flight with a resounding 4-0 opening day win at Huddersfield. There followed a 1-0 victory over Brentford before Nottingham Forest (2-1 at the Goldsands Stadium) and Blackburn Rovers (3-2 at Ewood Park) inflicted successive defeats upon Eddie Howe's team. In fact, Rovers scored their three goals in 11 first-half minutes to stun the Cherries. A 1-1 draw at Norwich City ended the first month of league activity, while at the same time, the Cherries made progress in the League Cup, beating Exeter City (2-0) and Northampton Town (3-0). The five league games played in September produced only one win – 2-0 at home to Wigan Athletic. Defeats came against Leeds United (3-1 at home) and Derby County (2-0 away), when Cherries goalkeeper Lee Camp was sent off with the scoreline blank. 1-1 draws came against Rotherham United (home) and Watford (away), and the Cherries had five players yellow-carded against the Hornets, while Cardiff City were knocked out of the League Cup, beaten 3-0 in South Wales.

TERRIFIC MONTH

October turned out to be a terrific month. Five games played, five wins, four of them in the league, at Bolton Wanderers 2-1 (despite Yann Kermorgant seeing red), versus 1-0 at home to Charlton Athletic, Reading 3-0, also at home, and 8-0 against Birmingham City at St Andrews – although Blues defender David Edgar was red-carded in the seventh minute. And for good measure, Premier League side West Bromwich Albion were knocked out of the League Cup, 2-1 at the Goldsands Stadium, in front of 11,296 fans. Riding high at this stage in the campaign, the Cherries were undefeated throughout November, beating Brighton 3-2 at home (eight players were booked in this rough encounter) and ten-man Sheffield Wednesday 2-0 away, while drawing 0-0 at Middlesbrough and 2-2 at home to Ipswich Town, and lowly Millwall. And it got even better in December with five more League victories being recorded – over nine-man Wolves 2-1 at Molineux, Cardiff City 5-3 at home (four goals were scored in five minutes either side of half-time), Blackpool 6-1 at Bloomfield Road, Fulham 2-0 at home and 2-0 at Millwall. who finished with ten men while seven other players received yellow cards. Unfortunately the Cherries succumbed to Liverpool in the League Cup, beaten 3-1 at home in front of 11,347 fans – the biggest crowd of the season.

MIXED JANUARY

Bournemouth played six more games in January, losing three of them, two in the league – 2-1 at home to ten-man Norwich City and 1-0 away to Leeds United, who were also down to ten. They also slipped gracefully out of the FA Cup, losing 2-1 away to the eventual finalists Aston Villa in round four – after Rotherham had been crushed 5-1 at Millmoor in the previous round. The Cherries, however, beat the Millers 2-0 in the league and also defeated Watford by the same score to keep themselves firmly in the promotion race. The Hornets had Italian defender Gabriele Angella sent off after 65 seconds. Unfortunately the results didn't go according to plan in February. It was a bad month all round. Bournemouth won one of six league games (3-1 at Wigan), drew 2-2 and 1-1 at home to Derby County and Huddersfield respectively, lost 3-1 at Brentford and went down 2-1 at Nottingham Forest before being held 0-0 at home by Blackburn. Said manager Howe, 'There's nothing to worry about. We will stick to our gameplan.' And true to his word, the Cherries did just that. Four wins came in March, three at home against Wolves (2-1), Blackpool (4-0 with a Brett Pitman treble) and Middlesbrough (3-0, two penalties scored) plus a 5-1 drubbing of ten-man Fulham at Craven Cottage, in front of the TV cameras. The other game ended 1-1 at Cardiff.

ALL TO PLAY FOR

So it was all to play for going into April. The Cherries knew what they had to do. They had seven games remaining and had to be at their best in every one. Five wins would see them up, but with Watford, Middlesbrough, Norwich, Derby, Ipswich, Brentford and Wolves all in with a chance of making the play-offs at least, the Cherries wanted automatic promotion, nothing less. They started with a vital 1-1 draw at Portman Road, loanee Kenwyne Jones heading an 82nd-minute equaliser – their 100th goal of the season. They then ran up three wins on the bounce, beating ten-man Birmingham 4-2 at home (after being 2-0 down), Brighton 2-0 away and Reading 1-0, also on the road. Unfortunately two points were dropped in their penultimate home game of the season against Sheffield Wednesday, who equalised at 2-2 with a 93rd-minute penalty. But nine days later, in front of almost 11,000 home fans, and millions more watching live on Sky Sports, the Cherries knew that victory over Bolton Wanderers would see them effectively win promotion to the Premier League – Watford had got there 48 hours earlier. Howe's men were never going to lose against the Trotters. It was the most important game in the club's 116-year history – and on a night to remember, and despite Yann Kermorgant missing a penalty, the Cherries won 3-0 with goals from Marc Pugh, Matt Ritchie and Callum Wilson. Some sarcastic pundits up and down the country said after the game, 'Don't celebrate yet, Charlton might just spoil the party by beating you 18-0 in the last game of the season at The Valley.' No way, Jose!

CHAMPIONS OF THE CHAMPIONSHIP

So, with one game remaining, it was all to play for with regards to who would win the Championship title. And it was the Cherries who took the star prize with a 3-0 win at Charlton while Watford were held 1-1 at home by Sheffield Wednesday. The Cherries had won the league by a single point (90 to 89). The players and officials celebrated promotion to the Premier League with an open-top bus parade through the town of Bournemouth on Bank Holiday Monday, 4 May. It was estimated that 60,000 fans (most of them clad in red and black) lined the route along the sea front from Boscombe to Bournemouth. Open-top bus parades have become a regular tradition in Bournemouth following the Cherries' two recent promotions from League 2 in 2010 and League 1 in 2013. Chairman Jeff Mostyn said, 'Eddie [Howe], Jason [Tindall], the players and myself have gone on record numerous times to thank the fans for their support, The backing we have received home and away has been truly incredible, And the fans have played their part in an unforgettable season. It is only fitting that the coaches and players get the opportunity to show their appreciation, and we are looking forward to celebrating an incredible achievement with thousands and thousands of supporters.'

2014/15 FACTS

The Cherries won 26, drew 12 and lost eight of their 46 league games. Their home record was played 23, won 13, drawn seven and lost three, while away it was 23-13-5-5. A total of 98 league goals were scored, 50 away for the first time. The home tally of 48 was the highest since 1957/58 when 54 were scored. Only 49 goals were conceded, 20 on the road, the second lowest in the club's history, beating the 15 given away in 1981/82. The 13 away wins was a new club record, beating the previous best of 11, set in 1947/48 (from 21 games), 1981/82, 2004/05 and 2012/13. The total of five away defeats was the club's second-lowest; they suffered three in 1981/82. The seasonal points tally of 90 was the second-best behind the 97 gained in 1986/87. The club's average home league attendance was 10,307 (aggregate 237,077 from 23 games played). The biggest turnout was 11,318 v. Norwich City; the lowest 8,460 v. Rotherham United. Steve Cook, captain Tommy Elphick and Matt Ritchie appeared in all 46 league games. Ritchie also starred in five cup ties to Cook's three. Callum Wilson made 45 league appearances, Harry Arter 43, Charlie Daniels, Simon Francis and Marc Pugh 42 each, Andrew Surman 41, Yann Kermorgant 38 (12 as a substitute), Artur Boruc 37 and Brett Pitman 34. Manager Howe used 24 different players in the league during the season. Wilson top-scored with 23 goals (20 in the league); Kermorgant netted 17 (15 league), Ritchie 15 (all league) and Pitman 14 (13 league).

SEASON 2015/016

Manager Eddie Howe arranged six friendly matches prior to the start of the club's first-ever season in the top flight of English football against Philadelphia Union/USA (a), Exeter City (a), Nantes/France (a), Yeovil Town (a), Cardiff City (h) and FC Hoffenheim/Germany (a). Then, during August 2015, the Cherries contested their first three Premier League fixtures, losing 1-0 at home to Aston Villa; going down by the same score at Liverpool (an unlucky defeat this) before registering their first-ever top-flight victory, 4-3 at West Ham United with a Callum Wilson hat-trick. They also won 4-0 at Hartlepool in a League Cup-tie. Said defender Tommy Elphick: 'It was a tough start, but all Premier League matches will be tough, won't they?' The Mansion Group agreed to be Bournemouth's Premier League shirt sponsor for the season.

FORMATION AND FOUNDATION

There was a Bournemouth football club as early as 1875, but the present one rose out of the remnants of the Boscombe St John's club which was initially formed in the summer of 1889. However, that club (then St John's Institute) dissolved ten years later and, following a meeting at a house in Gladstone Road, reformed in late 1899 as Boscombe FC, entering the local Boscombe and District Junior League. The club changed its name to Bournemouth and Boscombe Athletic FC in 1923 and since 1972 it has been known as AFC Bournemouth.

BOSCOMBE FC

Although the exact date of the club's foundation is not known, it is believed that it came into being in mid-1899. In the first season (1899/1900) Boscombe competed in the local District Junior League and also in the Hampshire Junior Cup. During the first two campaigns the club's home ground was on Castlemain Avenue, Pokesdown, from where they moved, in their third season, to King's Park, before the club graduated to senior amateur football in 1905. In the summer of 1910, president Mr J.E. Cooper-Deans negotiated a long lease on wasteland next to Kings Park and with their first 'own' ground – named Dean Court after the benefactor – the club continued to thrive and dominated the local football scene. Boscombe FC changed its name to Bournemouth and Boscombe FC in 1923, in readiness for their first season in the Football League.

FIRST PROFESSIONAL

Centre-forward Harry Baven Penton was the club's first professional footballer. Born in Boscombe in March 1890, he scored 85 goals in two seasons for Pokesdown (60 in 1909/10) and 26 for Boscombe before moving through the New Forest to Southampton in February 1911. He made his debut for Saints at Crystal Palace within a week and netted on his home debut at The Dell in his next match against Brentford. Penton, strong and mobile, returned to Boscombe in January 1912 for a fee of £10 to become the club's first professional, earning 30 shillings (£1.50) a week. In September 1912, having scored 12 FA Cup goals for the Cherries, he returned to The Dell, but made only one further appearance for Southampton before rejoining the Cherries. He moved to Eastleigh Athletic in 1914 and remained there until 1928, playing as goalkeeper rather than centre-forward. It is believed Penton died circa 1965 in Southampton.

INTO THE SOUTHERN LEAGUE

At the Football League's AGM in the summer of 1920, the Third Division was formed, meaning that several teams from the south of England became founder members, but not Boscombe, who were given membership of the Southern League. Thankfully, over the next three years, the team did very well and, in the summer of 1923, gained entry to the Football League Third Division South.

EARLY YEARS OF LEAGUE FOOTBALL

Initially Bournemouth struggled in the Football League, finishing next to bottom in the Third Division South table in their first season of 1923/24, winning only 11 games out of 42 played and scoring 40 goals, while conceding 65. They moved up one place to 20th in 1924/25, finished eighth in 1925/26, edged up to seventh in 1926/27, but slipped down to 14th in 1927/28. The team eventually established themselves as a solid, well organised side. And, indeed, the Cherries held their place in the Third Division until 1970 – the longest continuous membership in the third tier of any club.

FIRST SEASON STATS

The first Third Division South game played by Bournemouth was against Swindon Town (away) on 25 August 1923. The Cherries, who lost 2-1 in front of 10,000 spectators, fielded these 11 players for this historic encounter: Heron (goal), Wingham and Lamb (full-backs), Butt, C.

Smith and Voisey (half backs), Miller, Lister, Davey, Simpson and Robinson (forwards). Scotsman Jim Lister, formerly of Hearts, had the pleasure and, indeed, the honour of scoring the Cherries' first league goal. As it transpired, Bournemouth didn't have a very happy first season of league football and, at the end of the 1923/24 campaign, their record was disappointing, reading:

Venue	P	W	D	L	F	A	Pts
Home	21	6	8	7	19	19	20
Away	21	5	3	13	21	46	13
Totals	42	11	11	20	40	65	33

Position: 21st out of 22; only Queen's Park Rangers (31 points) finished below the Cherries in the table. Appearances/goals: Joe Armstrong 29 (2 goals), Wilf Budden 8 (1), Len Butt 42, Hugh Davey 34 (20), George Donowa 1, Horace Harrison 3, Alex Heron 24, Jimmy Lamb 42, Billy Leitch 33, Jim Lister 28 (7), Herbert Lock 13, Ken Marshall 2, Joe Miller 38, Foster Robinson 32 (1), Edgar Saxton 26, Albert Simpson 12 (3), Charlie Smith 37, Jim Tait 12 (4), Bill Voisey 26 (3), Harry Walker 1, Jim Whelpton 1 and Harry Wingham 18. Biggest wins: 3-1 v. QPR (h) and 4-3 v. Bristol Rovers (away). Heaviest defeats: 4-2 v. Brentford (home) and 5-0 v. Brighton (away). In the FA Cup the Cherries failed to reach the first round proper.

FOOTBALL LEAGUE RECORD: 1923-2015

This is Bournemouth's record in the Football League from 1923/24 to 2014/15, not including the void games of 1939/40 or any play-off matches.

Venue	P	W	D	L	F	A
Home	1914	975	521	418	3215	1909
Away	1914	469	492	953	2053	3125
Totals	3828	1444	1013	1371	5268	5034

The Cherries have amassed a grand total of 4,472 points. The three points for a win rule was introduced for the 1981/82 season.

CHERRIES' 25-YEAR LEAGUE RECORD

Season	Division	P	W	D	L	F	A	Pts	Pos.
1990/91	Third	46	19	13	14	58	58	70	9th
1991/92	Third	46	20	11	15	52	48	71	8th
1992/93	Second	46	12	17	17	45	52	53	17th
1993/94	Second	46	14	15	17	51	59	57	17th
1994/95	Second	46	13	11	22	49	69	50	19th

1995/96	Second	46	16	10	20	51	70	58	14th
1996/97	Second	46	15	15	16	43	45	60	16th
1997/98	Second	46	18	12	16	57	52	66	9th
1998/99	Second	46	21	13	12	63	41	76	7th
1999/2000	Second	46	16	9	21	59	62	57	16th
2000/01	Second	46	20	13	13	79	55	73	7th
2001/02	Second	46	10	14	22	56	71	44	21st
2002/03	Third	46	20	14	12	60	48	74	4th
2003/04	Second	46	17	15	14	56	51	66	9th
2004/05	FL 1	46	20	10	16	77	64	70	8th
2005/06	FL 1	46	12	19	15	49	53	55	17th
2006/07	FL 1	46	13	13	20	50	64	52	19th
2007/08	FL 1	46	17	7	22	62	72	48	21st
2008/09	FL 2	46	17	12	17	59	51	46	21st
2009/10	FL 2	46	25	8	13	61	44	83	2nd
2010/11	FL 1	46	19	14	13	75	54	71	6th
2011/12	FL 1	46	15	13	18	48	52	58	11th
2012/13	FL 1	46	24	11	11	76	53	83	2nd
2013/14	FL C	46	18	12	16	67	66	66	10th
2014/15	FL C	46	26	12	8	98	45	90	1st

Ten points were deducted in 2007/08 and 17 points in 2008/09.

FOOTBALL LEAGUE STATS AND FACTS

Here are the seasonal stats, facts and records achieved by the Cherries in league football; not including play-offs and the three games played in 1939/40:
- Most home wins: 19 in 1986/87 (23 games)
- Most away wins: 13 in 2014/15 (23 games)
- Most wins home and away: 29 in 1986/87 (46 games)
- Fewest home wins: six in 1923/24 (21 games)
- Fewest away wins: one in 1927/28 (21 games) and 2001/02 (23 games)
- Lowest home goals scored: 19 in 1923/24 (21 games)
- Lowest home goals conceded: 11 (23 games) in 1998/99
- Lowest away goals conceded: 13 in 1977/78 and 1978/79 (23 games)
- Most goals scored at home: 57 in 1956/57 (23 games)
- Most goals scored away: 50 in 2014/15 (23 games)
- Most goals scored home and away: 98 in 2014/15 (46 games)
- Most goals conceded at home: 39 in 1960/61 (23 games)
- Most goals conceded away: 65 in 1933/34 (21 games)
- Most goals conceded home and away: 102 (37/65) in 1933/34 (46 games)
- Most home defeats: ten in 1994/95 and 2001/02 (23 games)
- Fewest home defeats: none in 1962/63 (23 games)

- Most away defeats: 17 in 1933/34 (23 games)
- Most home draws: 12 in 1962/63 (23 games)
- Most away draws: ten on six occasions, the last in 2002/03 (23 games)
- Most draws in total (home and away): 19 in 1981/82 and 2005/06 (46 games)
- Most points gained (home and away): 97 in 1986/87 (46 games)
- Most points gained (home and away): 57 in 1947/48 (21 games)
- Lowest points tally (home and away): 27 in 1933/34 (42 games)
- Lowest points tally (home and away): 38 in 1965/66 (46 games)
- Fewest points gained at home: 20 in 1923/24 (21 games)
- Fewest points gained away: six in 1933/34 (21 games)
- Fewest points gained away: 11 in 1953/54 (23 games)
- Identical record (home and away): 11 wins, six draws, six defeats in 2009/10
- First time 50 goals scored at home: 54 in 1928/29 (21 games)
- Unbeaten away: 20 matches (11 wins, nine draws) in 1981/82
- Cherries scored more away goals than at home (21/19) in 1923/24: 2011/12 (25/23) and 2014/15 (50/48).
- Between 1946/47 and 1964/65, the Cherries' points tally did not drop below 40.
- The 1,000th league game was played in 1953/54; the 2,000th in 1975/76; the 2,500th in 1986/87 and the 3,000th in 1996/97.
- The Cherries need 25 more wins to reach the milestone of 1,000 in the league, while eight draws are required to top 500 away from home.

DEAN COURT FIRSTS

The first football match played at Dean Court was between Boscombe and Southampton's reserve XI on 31 December 1910. Barely 500 spectators witnessed the 1-1 draw. The first Football League game staged on the ground was Bournemouth against Swindon Town on 1 September 1923 and this also finished in a draw, 0-0, in front of 7,000 fans. The first floodlit game played at Dean Court, on 27 September 1961, was a Third Division fixture when Bournemouth beat Northampton Town 3-2.

OUT AT HIGHBURY

Ipswich Town knocked Bournemouth out of the FA Cup in a first round second replay at Highbury in December 1952. After drawing twice with the Tractormen, 2-2 at Portman Road and by the same score at Dean Court, the Cherries lost 3-2 at Arsenal's ground in North London (see Longest Ties).

TESTIMONIALS

Over the years, a Bournemouth team has played in several testimonial matches, for players, club officials and various charities. Here are details of some of these 'friendly' encounters:

31 Dec 1949 ... Bournemouth 3 Notts County 0..............(Ken Bird)*
28 Oct 1970.... Bournemouth 5 Top Ten XI 4.................(Jack Stamps)**
13 Mar 1973... Bournemouth 3 West Ham United 3 ....(Bill Kitchener)
3 Apr 1974...... Bournemouth 1 Wolves 1........................(For three players)†
19 Jan 1976..... Bournemouth 0 Norwich City 2..............(Arthur Cunliffe)
5 May 1980 .... Bournemouth 1 Tottenham Hotspur 2...(Keith Miller)
14 Jul 2014...... Poole Town 2 Bournemouth Youth 0......('Taffy' Richardson)

* This was a Third Division South League match (see under Huge Benefit).
** The result of this game differs in some reports: the final score could have been after a penalty shootout. †This was a joint testimonial for three players – Tommy Mitchinson, John Meredith and Arthur Cunliffe.

EVER-PRESENTS

The first two players to appear in every Football League game for the Cherries in the same season were wing-half Len Butt and full-back Jim Lamb, both in 1923/24. A further nine players were ever-presents for the Cherries up to Second World War (ending with the 1938/39 season), and these included the first goalkeepers Peter Sevitch (1930/31) and Dick Mellors (1936/37). In the first Football League season after the war (1946/47), four players appeared in all 42 Third Division South games for the Cherries – Kenny Bird, Fred Marsden, Joe Sanaghan and Fred Wilson. Interestingly, all these long-established professionals each received a benefit from the club before 1951. Marsden did not miss a single game in 1947/48 either, while Bird was an ever-present for a second time in 1948/49. Captain Ian Cox never missed a game in 1997/98 and 1998/99, while goalkeepers Jimmy Glass and Mark Overdale were also ever-presents in the latter two campaigns respectively. Striker James Hayter was an ever-present in 2005/06 and likewise Brett Pitman in 2009/10. Wade Elliott featured in all 46 league games in 2001/02, goalkeeper Neil Moss was an ever-present in 2003/04, and three players – Steve Cook, skipper Tommy Elphick and Matt Ritchie – appeared in all 46 Championship games in 2014/15.Over the last 65 years or so it has been very rare for any one player to line up in every league game in a single season, certainly since the substitute rule was introduced in 1965 and more so since the club enhanced the first team squad.

FIRST PRESIDENT

Local businessman Mr J. C. Nutt was the first president of Boscombe Football Club, for the 1899/1900 season. He was followed into office by another local businessman, Mr J.E. Cooper-Dean, the man responsible for 'building' the club's ground, Dean Court.

AMATEUR TRIO

In the late 1950s, Bournemouth played three amateur clubs in quick succession in the FA Cup. They lost 3-1 at Tooting and Mitcham in November 1958, won 3-2 at Walthamstow Avenue in November 1959 and beat Enfield 5-1 away a month later.

FIRST GAME

Boston United's first Football League game resulted in a 2-2 home draw with Bournemouth on 10 August 2002. A crowd of 4,184 at the York Street Stadium saw Irishman Shaun Maher and Brian Stock bag the Cherries' goals.

FIRST TROPHIES

In May 1946, Bournemouth defeated Walsall 1-0 in the Third Division South Cup Final, the club's first major trophy success (see under Wartime Football). Some 45 years later, the Cherries won their first 'competitive' knockout tournament – the Associate Members Cup – by beating Hull City 2-1 at Boothferry Park before a crowd of 6,544. Paul Morrell scored the winning goal.

FA CUP GIANTKILLERS IN 1956/57

The Cherries hit the sporting headlines in 1956/57 courtesy of a terrific run in the FA Cup, despite being handed some of the hardest draws imaginable. After beating non-league side Burton Albion 8-0 (Ollie Norris scored a hat-trick), Swindon Town 1-0 and Accrington Stanley 2-0 in rounds one, two and three respectively, the Cherries were paired with Wolverhampton Wanderers in round four. Lying third in the top flight at the time, Wolves had won the First Division title in 1953/54, finished runners-up in 1954/55 and came third in 1955/56. In front of 41,752 fans at Molineux, the Cherries produced a great performance, beating Stan Cullis's team 1-0 to earn a home tie in the fifth round against the team in second place in the First Division, Tottenham Hotspur. Blackheath-born left-winger Reg Cutler, once of West Bromwich Albion, returned to the

Black Country to net the all-important goal in the 43rd minute which stunned Wolves. Early in the game Cutler, challenging the Wolves and England goalkeeper Bert Williams, collided with an upright at the South Bank end of the ground, causing it to snap in two near the base. It took seven minutes to repair the post. In the next round, the Cherries produced another stunning display to knock out Spurs 3-1 before 25,892 fans at Dean Court. In fact, such was the demand for tickets for this tie, when they went on sale during a reserve game against Aldershot, a crowd of 19,531 turned up at Dean Court for a Football Combination fixture. Olly Norris, Stan Newsham and Nelson Stiffle's 25-yarder booked the Cherries a place in the sixth round of the competition for the first time in the club's history. And their reward was another money-spinning home tie against Manchester United – the top side in the country at the time, and managed by Matt Busby. Sadly, the dream of a Wembley final ended there and then, albeit in controversial circumstances, as United won a closely-fought game 2-1 before a record 28,799 crowd. Brian Bedford gave the Cherries a deserved first-half lead, netting from close range. United's equaliser by Johnny Berry looked suspiciously offside and their second goal, also from the boot of Berry, came from a debatable penalty, after the referee decided that Mick Lyons had handled inside the area. Despite this defeat, Bournemouth grabbed the imagination of the nation's football lovers and for their bold and noble efforts, deservedly received 'The Giant Killers Cup' for that season. Busby's United went on to win the First Division title, but lost 2-1 to Aston Villa in the FA Cup Final.

MORE FA CUP FACTS

Bournemouth entered the FA Cup competition for the very first time in 1909/10. Playing initially in the preliminary qualifying rounds, they defeated the local gas works team 2-1 in a home replay before losing 3-2 away to Poole. The following season, they won 4-2 at Weymouth and 4-1 in a replay at Poole, before succumbing 1-0 against Babbacombe (Torquay). After failing to compete in the competition in 1911/12, the Cherries ran up two excellent wins of 6-1 over Portland and 7-1 against Gosport the following season before exiting at the hands of the First Kings Royal Regiment team from Lancaster. In 1919/20, the Cherries missed two penalties, yet still blitzed Poole St Mary's 9-0 in a qualifying tie, but again failed to make the first round proper. Six years later, in 1925/26, the Cherries reached the fourth round for the very first time. They beat Merthyr Town 3-0 and Brentford 2-1 in their opening two games, and knocked out Reading in round three, before drawing 2-2 with Bolton Wanderers, only to lose the replay 5-2 at Burnden Park to the eventual trophy winners. In round one of three successive seasons – 1935–38 – Bournemouth were drawn against non-league opponents. They won all three ties, beating, in turn, Walthamstow Avenue 8-1 in a replay, Harwich 5-1 and Dartford 6-0, also in a replay. Bournemouth knocked both Bristol clubs out of the competition in 1938/39 – defeating City 2-1 at home and Rovers 3-0 away. The Cherries came a mighty cropper against non-leaguers Lovells Athletic in 1945/46 – the only season when FA Cup ties (up to the semi-final stage) have been played over two legs. Both clubs won their home games, Lovells 4-1 and the Cherries 3-2, but it was the Welsh club who went through, 6-4 on aggregate. After successive 4-2 wins over Exeter City and Aldershot in 1946/47, the Cherries were ousted in round three by holders Derby County in front of a Dean Court crowd of 18,438. Bournemouth lost 2-1 at home to Wolves in a third round tie in 1947/48 and crashed out 6-0 at holders Manchester United at the same stage the following season. In 1951/52, Bournemouth got humbled 6-1 at Southend United in round one and were beaten 1-0 at home by holders West Bromwich Albion in 1954/55. Over a ten-year period from 1957/58, Bournemouth beat Enfield 5-1, Oswestry 5-1, Yeovil 3-1, Gravesend & Northfleet 7-0, Weymouth 4-1, Bath City 5-3, Welton Rovers 3-0 and Walthamstow Avenue 3-1 and 3-2, but also lost 3-1 to Tooting & Mitcham, 3-0 at home to Margate, 7-0 at Burnley, and 4-1 at Liverpool and Northampton Town. During the 1970s, apart from battering Margate 11-0, the Cherries had good cup wins against Oxford City 8-1, Cambridge United 5-1 and Southwick 5-0, but they suffered a few 'hard-to-take' defeats, among them 1-0 at home to Yeovil, 2-1 versus Wycombe, 2-0 against Hereford United and 3-0 at Newport County. After ousting Walsall 4-0 and minnows Windsor & Eton 2-0 in a replay, Bournemouth claimed a famous third-round victory over holders Manchester United in January 1984. Managed at the time by Harry Redknapp, the Cherries won 2-0 at Dean Court in front of 15,000 spectators, Milton Graham and Ian Thompson the scorers. However, in the next round, Bournemouth lost 2-0 at Middlesbrough. In 1984/85, United gained revenge with a 3-0 victory in round three at Old Trafford before 32,080 fans. Earlier, the Cherries had knocked out non-league sides Kettering Town and Dartford, both after replays. Moving on, in 1988/89 a crowd of 52,422 saw Bournemouth lose a fifth round tie at Old Trafford 1-0, Brian McClair scoring in the first half. In January 1991, Bournemouth crashed out in the fourth round, hammered by neighbours Portsmouth 5-1 at Fratton Park. Guy Whittingham scored four of Pompey's goals. After holding Newcastle United to a 0-0 draw at Dean Court in the third round in 1991/92, the replay at St James' Park was abandoned through fog after just 17 minutes. The re-arranged fixture, however, was exciting and following a 2-2 scoreline after 120 minutes, it was Bournemouth who progressed, winning the penalty shootout 4-3. Alas, in the next round, the Cherries lost 3-0 at Ipswich. Bournemouth were knocked out by Brentford in successive seasons, 1995/96 and 1996/97 – losing 1-0 at home and 2-0 away respectively. Future manager Eddie Howe struck Bournemouth's 34th-minute goal which knocked West Bromwich Albion out in the third round in January 1999 before a crowd of 10,881 at Dean Court. And the Cherries were eliminated from the competition by non-league side Tamworth in the second round in 2005/06 and went out to Blyth Spartans three seasons later. Since then Bournemouth have had mixed results in the competition, achieving nothing special, while at the same time, suffering few embarrassments.

HEAVY FA CUP DEFATS

The Cherries' heaviest defeat in the FA Cup is 7-0 – in the fourth round at Sheffield Wednesday in January 1932 and a third round replay at Burnley in January 1965.

CHERRIES' FA CUP RECORD

Bournemouth's record in the FA Cup competition since 1923/24 to 2014/15 inclusive:

Venue	P	W	D	L	F	A
Home	130	78	28	24	285	126
Away	125	33	31	61	152	220
Totals	255	111	59	85	437	346

*Replays played on a neutral ground have been placed in the 'away' category.

Prior to entering the Football League in 1923, the Cherries' cup record is unconfirmed, but details reveal these statistics:

Venue	P	W	D	L	F	A
Home	7	5	2	0	28	6
Away	12	2	1	9	14	20
Totals	19	7	3	9	42	26

A REAL FRIENDLY!

Spanish giants Real Madrid visited Bournemouth for a pre-season friendly in July 2013 and a record 11,772 crowd at the Goldsands Stadium saw the nine-time European champions win in style, 6-0. The result was no surprise. Cristiano Ronaldo scored two first-half goals, one a 30-yard special and, after the break, Sammy Khedira, Gonzalo Higuain, Angel di Maria and Carlos Casemiro added four more. Manager Eddie Howe said afterwards, 'The supporters will remember the game for the rest of their lives despite the result. The players were down-hearted, but felt they took the game to Real Madrid for the first 20 minutes. It was disappointing to lose so heavily, because we have a team that isn't used to losing.'

FIRST INTERNATIONAL

In February 1930, inside-forward Sammy Beswick made his England amateur international debut in a 2-1 win over Wales in Aberystwyth – thus becoming the first Bournemouth player to win a cap at any level. Beswick, who scored 11 goals in 56 league appearances for the Cherries from 1929–32, later played for Poole Town.

RED-FACED CHERRIES

Bournemouth defender Neil Young was sent off twice in four weeks in 2004 – taking an early bath in the away league games against Hull City on 7 August and Brentford on 4 September. On New Year's Eve 2015, Young was dismissed for third time in the away league encounter with Southend United. Jeff Goulding saw red in the away League 2 fixture against Grimsby Town in March 2010, having come on as a second-half substitute in the Cherries' 3-2 defeat.

GOAL MACHINE

Frank Fidler, born in 1924, joined Manchester United at the age of 17 while serving with the Irish Guards during the Second World War. After the hostilities he scored 179 goals in non-league football for Witton Albion and netted six times in 22 games for Leeds United before joining Bournemouth in December 1952. Fidler went on to bag 31 goals in 61 league games for the Cherries up to his retirement in May 1954.

GOALSCORING DEFENDER

As of May 2015, full-back Ian Harte was lying third in the all-time list of scoring defenders in the Premier League. He had netted 28 goals in the top flight (all for Leeds United) behind Chelsea's John Terry (39) and the former Everton, Portsmouth and West Ham left-back David Unsworth (38). Terry's total is by far the best return, as it doesn't contain a penalty or free kick.

FOUR-TIME DEBUTANT

Mark Nightingale became the first player to make his debut in all four divisions of the Football League while still a teenager. He was 19 when he started his career with Bournemouth, appearing in a 1-0 Third Division victory at Tranmere Rovers in August 1974. He then had an outing in the

Fourth Division, also for the Cherries at Hartlepool United in August 1975, before following up with further games in the Second and First Divisions with Crystal Palace and Norwich City respectively. Born in Salisbury in February 1957, Nightingale, after playing for Bulova in Hong Kong, returned to Dean Court for a second spell in 1982 before ending his career with Peterborough United in 1988. He made 312 Football League appearances overall (199 for the Cherries), scoring 11 goals.

RUNNERS-UP BUT NOT PROMOTED

In 1947/48, with manager Harry Lowe at the helm, Bournemouth battled long and hard before finishing runners-up in the Third Division South table behind Queens Park Rangers. But with only one club promoted in those days, the Cherries missed out on a place in the second tier of English football by just four points. The London club completed the double over Bournemouth, winning both games 1-0. The following season (1948/49) Bournemouth took third place in the Third Division South, behind champions Swansea Town and second-placed Reading. They had nothing to moan about this time as the Welsh club were ten points better off at the death.

MIXED SIXTIES

Bournemouth started the 1960s disappointingly, finishing sixth from bottom in the Third Division, just two points clear of relegation. They improved tremendously the following season, and claimed third place behind Portsmouth and Grimsby Town, missing promotion by three points. In season 1962/63 they took fifth place on 52 points, with champions Northampton Town (62), Swindon Town (58), Port Vale (54) and Coventry City (53) above them. Bournemouth then went one better in 1963/64, claiming fourth spot with 56 points, just four fewer than the top two, Coventry City and Crystal Palace, and two less than third-placed Watford. This was a close-run contest as the Cherries beat all the teams above them at Dean Court, but picked up only one point against those same clubs away, at Coventry. In 1964/65, the Cherries fell down the table to 11th place. They finished even lower in 1965/66, ending up seventh from bottom. And then, in 1966/67, they avoided the drop by just two points, ending up in 20th spot before improving considerably in 1967/68 to occupy 13th place. The 1968/69 season was a pretty good one, as Bournemouth came fourth in the division behind champions Watford, Swindon Town and Luton Town. But the Cherries were never really in with a shout of gaining promotion; they were always off the pace and finished 13 points behind both the Hornets and the Robins, and were ten adrift of the Hatters. The last season of the 1960s (1969/70) saw Bournemouth relegated. They finished fourth from bottom and went down with Stockport County, Barrow and Southport. They won just 12 of their 46 matches, lost 19 and scored only 48 goals, while conceding 71. In the ten league seasons of the 1960s, Bournemouth finished in a different position on nine occasions: 1960/61 (19th), 1961/62 (third), 1962/63 (fifth), 1963/64 (fourth), 1964/65 (11th), 1965/66 (18th), 1966/67 (20th), 1967/68 (13th), 1968/69 (fourth again) and 1969/70 (21st).

PROMOTION GLORY

Bournemouth have so far gained promotion on six occasions – in 1970/71, 1981/82, 1986/87, 2009/10, 2012/13 and, of course, in 2014/15. In 1970/71, as runners-up, they climbed into the Third Division with champions Notts County, who won the title by nine points (69-60). Eleven years later, in 1981/82, under David Webb, the Cherries, with 88 points, finished fourth in the Fourth Division and won promotion. Sheffield United (96), Bradford City (91) and Wigan Athletic (91) were the top three. Their next successful promotion campaign, in 1986/87, saw the Cherries win the Third Division championship by three points from Middlesbrough (97-94) with Swindon Town a distant third (87). Harry Redknapp was in the hotseat and he had a decent team which won 29 out of 46 league games, scored 76 goals and conceded only 40. In 2009/10, with Eddie Howe in charge for the first time, Bournemouth came runners-up to Notts County in League 2 and, after being relegated, they did likewise in 2012/13, claiming second spot, a point behind champions Doncaster Rovers (84-83). Unbeaten in their last nine games, eight of which were won, the Cherries shot up from seventh to second in the space of six weeks, overtaking Brentford in the run-in. Then, with Howe in charge once again, came 2014/15 when the Cherries clinched a place in the Premier League for the first time in the club's history (See: Into the Premier League).

GOALS MILESTONE

Aston Villa became the first club to score 6,000 goals in the Football League when England winger Mark Walters netted in his side's 1-1 draw with Bournemouth at Villa Park in a Second Division match in October 1987.

RECORD GOAL TALLY

A record number of goals (209) were scored in the 44 league games played on Saturday 1 February 1936. The First Divisionsaw 46 goals scored, with 46 in the Second Division, 49 in the Third Division South and 68 in the Third Division North. Bournemouth and Cardiff City contributed eight – drawing 4-4 at Dean Court.

FOUR GOALS TO NO AVAIL!

Merthyr Town centre-forward Jack Phillips scored four goals in a Third Division South game against Bournemouth in March 1927, but still finished on the losing side as the Cherries won 6-4 before 2,000 fans at the Welsh club's Penydarren Park ground.

FOOTBALL LEAGUE JUBILEE FUND MATCHES

To celebrate the jubilee of the Football League, Bournemouth played Devon neighbours Torquay United in home and away friendly matches at Dean Court and Plainmoor in successive seasons. In August 1938, a crowd of 3,000 saw the Cherries win their home match 1-0, and a year later, in August 1939, just over 1,600 spectators were present as the Gulls gained revenge with a 3-1 victory on their home patch. It is believed that for their home game against Torquay in 1938, the Bournemouth players wore numbered shirts for the first time in the club's history.

NOT QUITE THEIR SUNDAY BEST

The first Sunday Football League game played by Bournemouth was against lowly Southport at Haig Avenue on 24 February 1974. It ended in a 1-0 defeat, Alex Russell scoring the deciding goal in the second half in front of 2,719 spectators.

CHERRIES V. THE GLOVERS

Bournemouth's playing record against Yeovil Town on paper looks good:

P	W	D	L	F	A
21	12	5	4	33	19

There have been two FA Cup meetings: the Cherries won 3-1 in 1960/61 and the Glovers 1-0 in 1970/71. Both Johnstone's Paint Trophy matches resulted in wins for Bournemouth, 2-1 in 2009 and 3-1 in 2011 and, in a LDV Trophy game of 2003, Yeovil won 2-0. The Cherries have won seven of the 14 league encounters, including successive 3-0 home victories in 2012 and 2013. Yeovil have so far won just two. Defender Terrell Forbes, striker James Hayter and goalkeeper Gareth Stewart are three of the handful of players who have served with both clubs; Harry Lowe and David Webb managed at Dean Court and Huish Park, Trevor Finnigan was a Cherries player who became boss of the Glovers, and Alec Stock, who captained Yeovil in the 1930s, subsequently bossed Bournemouth in 1979/80.

ON HIGH GROUND

The Hawthorns, home of West Bromwich Albion, built in 1900, is the 'highest' Premier League/Football League ground in the UK – standing 551 feet above sea level. And Bournemouth have played there eight times. The Cherries first visited Baggies soil for a Wartime League Cup tie in March 1940, losing 3-1 in front of 7,619 fans. Then, prior to the start of the 1973/74 campaign. they beat Albion 1-0 in a friendly on 'high ground' before a crowd of 4,304. There have so far been five league games between the two clubs in the Black Country. Bournemouth lost 3-0 in September 1987 (attendance 7,749); drew 0-0 in October 1988 (7,248); drew again, 2-2, in December 1989 (8,568); crashed to a 4-0 defeat in January 1992 (10,932) and lost 2-1 in August 1992 (12,563). The Cherries also visited The Hawthorns in the first round League Cup-tie in August 2007, when the Baggies won 1-0 in front of 10,250 spectators.

CHERRIES IN THE LEAGUE CUP

During the late 1950s, the majority of the First and Second Division clubs equipped their grounds with floodlights. This opened up the opportunity to play midweek matches during the winter months, hence the Football League Cup was introduced for the 1960/61 season. Since its inception, the competition itself has had many guises. Known initially as The Football League Cup (1960–81), it then became The Milk Cup (1981–86); The Littlewoods Cup (1986–90); The Rumbelows Cup (1990–92); The Coca-Cola Cup (1992–98); The Worthington Cup (1998–2002); The Carling Cup (2002–2012) and, more recently, The Capital One Cup (2012–present). This is Bournemouth's record in the League Cup, 1960–2015:

Venue	P	W	D	L	F	A
Home	70	21	24	25	78	78
Away	77	13	25	39	70	115
Totals	147	34	49	64	148	193

* Penalty shootouts not included – games classed as draws.

LEAGUE CUP ACTION

Bournemouth, who entered the competition at the outset, received a bye in the first round in 1960/61, but went out at the second stage, beaten 2-0 at Crewe Alexandra in a replay after a 1-1 draw in front of almost 6,000 fans. The following season the Cherries recorded their first League Cup victory, defeating Torquay United 1-0 at Plainmoor, again in a replay, after a 2-2 draw. In August 1968 the Cherries suffered one of their heaviest home defeats, losing 6-1 to Southend United in the first round.

In 1975/76 the competition saw the introduction of two-legged ties, but the Cherries didn't get off to the greatest of starts, losing 4-1 on aggregate to Plymouth Argyle (2-0 and 2-1) in the opening round. Bournemouth's first round tie with Watford in 1969/70 went to three games before the Hornets won 2-1 in a second replay at Vicarage Road. There were three tough matches with Blackpool in 1972/73, the Seasiders eventually winning a second replay 2-1 at Villa Park. The Cherries were defeated at the third attempt by Sheffield Wednesday in 1973/74, but came good against Gillingham the following season, winning a first round second replay 2-1 at Brentford's Griffin Park. Bournemouth's second round clash with Hartlepool in 1974/75 went to four games (420+ minutes of action). After three draws (1-1, 2-2 and 1-1, the latter two both after extra time) 'Pool took the honours with a 1-0 victory in the fourth game. In 1982/83, the Cherries knocked out Plymouth Argyle in the first round (coming back from a 2-0 first leg deficit with a 3-0 victory at Dean Court), but then went out to Manchester United, losing 4-2 on aggregate. After a gutsy performance at Old Trafford where they lost 2-0, the Cherries battled hard and long to earn a 2-2 draw in the return leg to go out with their heads held high. The Cherries lost 5-0 on aggregate to Aldershot in a first round tie in 1984/85 and were dumped out of the competition by Coventry, 7-1 over two legs, in round two in 1988/89. Twelve months earlier, in 1987/88, plucky Bournemouth were eliminated 3-0 by Arsenal before 26,050 fans at Highbury. The Gunners reached the final, but lost 3-2 to Luton Town for whom Brian Stein, brother of future Cherry Mark, scored twice. In 1991/92, the Cherries beat Cardiff City 6-4 on aggregate to reach round two, winning 4-1 at home after losing 3-2 at Ninian Park. Unfortunately Bournemouth were eliminated in a penalty shootout by Charlton Athletic in 1999/2000, ousted by Brentford in the same way in 2002/03 and by Oxford United also from 12 yards in 2012/13, but they did win ties with shootouts against Blackburn in 2004/05 (after a 3-3 draw at Ewood Park) and Torquay United in 2005/06. West Bromwich Albion won 4-1 at Dean Court in 2011/12, after the Cherries had earlier recorded their biggest League Cup win, 5-0 over Dagenham & Redbridge with goals from Marc Pugh, Shaun Cooper, Warren Feeney and Lyle Taylor (2) before 3,681 fans. Bournemouth gained revenge over the Baggies in 2014/15, knocking the Premier League side out of the competition 2-1 at home, Callum Wilson scoring a dramatic late winner. Bournemouth failed to win a single League Cup game between 1963 and 1969, 1974 and 1978, and 1978 and 1983.

CUP GAMES GALORE

Bournemouth fulfilled 11 cup ties in 2002/03 – one in the League Cup, four in the Leyland DAF Vans Trophy and six in the FA Cup. They won five, drew four and lost two of these fixtures, scoring 18 goals and conceding 18. They were knocked out of the League Cup by Brentford on penalties. In 2011/12, the Cherries contested seven cup games which produced a total of 37 goals, 19 scored by opponents.

SPLASHED IN PAINT

Brentford 'splattered' Bournemouth 6-0 at Griffin Park in the Southern Section quarter-finals of the Johnstone's Paint Trophy in 2011/12.

NINE ON TARGET

Nine different players scored in the league game between Bournemouth and Plymouth Argyle at Dean Court in January 1975. Argyle won 7-3 with goals by Paul Mariner (2), Billy Rafferty, Hugh McAuley, John Delve, Colin Randall and Brian Johnson. John Wingate, Mike Green and Trevor Howard (own goal) netted for Bournemouth.

BIG, BIG MAN

The first (and seemingly only) 6ft 9in player to be registered as a professional with a Football League club is Bournemouth's reserve team goalkeeper Bill Carr, who was at Dean Court in 1924/25.

STRONG DEFENCE

In 1981/82, Bournemouth gained promotion from the Fourth Division on the back of an excellent defence which conceded only 30 goals in 46 matches (15 at home, 15 away). This same season also saw the Cherries draw a record 19 games. The defence gave away 35 goals in 1947/48 (13 at home); conceded 37 in 1971/72 (13 at home again), let in 41 in 1998/99 and shipped 45 in 2014/15. However, the back division conceded only 11 goals at Dean Court in 23 league matches in 1998/99 (a club record); 13 were leaked for a third time in 1976/77 and the defence gave away 14 in 1955/56 and 1986/87, 15 in 1963/64, 1970/71, 1997/98, 2008/09 and 16 in 1972/73, 1975/76, 1984/85 and 2009/10.

GOOD START FOR DAVEY

Hugh Davey netted half of Bournemouth's 40 goals in 1923/24, the club's first season of Third Division South football, despite missing eight matches. The Cherries scored in only 23 of the 42 games and finished the season next to bottom, a place above Queens Park Rangers. At the end of the day, just five points separated Bournemouth from 12th-placed Aberdare Athletic (38-33).

HUGE BENEFIT

In December 1949, Bournemouth granted goalkeeper Ken Bird a home league game as his testimonial match. Bird chose to celebrate the occasion against Notts County on New Year's Eve and a crowd of 22,651 turned up see the Cherries win 3-0 in what was Bird's 200th senior appearance for the club (See under: Testimonials).

WARTIME FOOTBALL

Bournemouth's playing record (all games) during the Second World War (FA Cup matches from the 1945/46 season are not included):

Season	P	W	D	L	F	A
1939/40	40	20	5	15	110	87
1940/41	29	9	4	16	64	99
1941/42	18	8	2	8	37	39
1945/46	39	17	8	14	92	71
Totals	126	54	19	53	303	296

WARTIME DISPATCHES

Bournemouth's first game after the declaration of the Second World War saw them draw 2-2 at home with Southampton on 16 September 1939. They lost their second game 2-1 at home to West Ham a week later before registering their first wartime win against Torquay United, 4-1 on 7 October. In that initial 1939/40 season, Reg Kirkham was Bournemouth's top scorer with 25 goals while Fred Marsden (38), Charlie Burke (35), John McDonald and Joe Sanaghan (34 each), and Tom Paton (31) made the most appearances. Guest forward Alec Cowan (29) and McDonald (25) played in most games in 1940/41 while another guest, Alf Whittingham, along with Cowan, starred in 17 and 16 matches respectively in 1941/42. Bournemouth did not play wartime football at senior level for three seasons, 1942–45, but on their return, in 1945/46, the top appearance-makers were Tom Paton (36), Kenny Bird (34), Fred Marsden and John McDonald (32) each, while John Thomas top-scored with 31 goals. And it was McDonald who netted Bournemouth's winning goal in the 1946 Third Division South Cup Final against Walsall in front of 19,715 fans at Stamford Bridge. The team that afternoon was: Bird; Marsden, Sanaghan; Woodward, Wilson, Gallacher; Currie, Paton, Kirkham, Tagg and McDonald. Future Wolves and England stars Johnny Hancocks and Dennis Wilshaw played for the Saddlers. In the space of a week, in February 1941, Bournemouth conceded ten goals in a Wartime League Cup tie. They lost 4-1 at Tottenham Hotspur in front of 3,412 fans and then crashed 6-1 in the return leg at Dean Court before a crowd of 1,982. After beating Plymouth Argyle 5-1 at Home Park in the first round of the same competition the previous season, the Cherries were defeated 3-1 by West Bromwich Albion in the second round at The Hawthorns (5-2 on aggregate). Among the 60-plus players who guested for Bournemouth during World War Two were future England internationals Wilf Mannion (Middlesbrough) and Jack Rowley (Manchester United; also an ex-Cherry); Scottish stars Matt Busby (Liverpool) and Sam Cowan (ex-Manchester City and Bradford City); England cricketers Bill Edrich (Chelmsford City) and Willie Watson (Huddersfield Town); goalkeepers Sam Bartram (Charlton Athletic), John Burke (Millwall), Ben Darling (Hull City), Norman Jones (Wrexham), George Tweedy (Grimsby Town) and Dave Whitehall (Gillingham); Welsh international Mal Griffiths (Leicester City); Bill Fielding (Cardiff City), England amateur international Lester Finch (Barnet), Harry Lowery (WBA), Dave McCulloch (Derby County), John McDonald (Wolves), Johnny Morrison (Spurs), Harry Phipps (Charlton), George Raynor (Aldershot), Tommy Rigg (Middlesbrough), John Simpson (Sheffield United), Alan Squires (Preston), Ellis Stuttard (Plymouth), Reg Swinfen (QPR), Jack Taylor (WBA), Oliver Tidman (Chelmsford City), George Tootill (Sheffield United), Reg Trim (Nottingham Forest) and Fred Westlake (Sheffield Wednesday), and Alf Whittingham (Bradford City). Other guests included David Bewley, Bob Bigg, Lewis Brook, Stan Dixon, Dick Foss, Charlie Gardiner, Harry Gray, Tom Hinchliffe, Jimmy 'Ned' Kelly, Maurice Lindley, Charlie Longdon, Ted Martin, Harry Oliver, Henry Picton, Eddie Platt, Maurice Priestley, Ernie Reid, Len Riches, John Robinson, George Rothery, ex-Cherries Eric Sibley and Dick Twiss, Harry Walker and Charlie Wilkinson. The top 15 appearance-makers for the Cherries during World War Two were John McDonald (93), Charlie Burke (85), Fred Marsden (71), Tommy Paton (68), Ken Bird (60), Patsy Gallacher (54), Joe Sanaghan (50), Bob Redfern (38), Jack Kirkham (35), Bob Young (33), Alec Cowan (29), Dick Twiss (29), Fred Wilson (28), John Thomas (25) and Alf Whittingham (24). The top wartime goalscorers were McDonald (43), Paton (39), Kirkham (33), Thomas (28) (plus three FA Cup goals), Burke (18), Bob Matthews (16), Gallacher (15), Redfern (15), Cowan (13) and Whittingham (12). Sadly, in 1944, Bournemouth's

Scottish-born left-half Peter Monaghan was killed in action while serving with the British Army in France. He was just 21 years old.

NICKNAMES

It is believed that AFC Bournemouth adopted their nickname, The Cherries, around 1910. Initially there were two conflicting stories as to how the club gained this pet name. Firstly it is said it came from the cherry-red striped shirts that the team wore, but perhaps more plausible, it derived from the club's ground – Dean Court – which was built adjacent to the Cooper-Dean estate, which encompassed numerous cherry orchards. During their respective careers, invariably most footballers get tagged with a nickname, some of them utterly stupid. Here are a few which were attached to certain Bournemouth stars: David 'Baldy' and 'Skin-head' Armstrong, Len 'Badger' Butt, Jimmy 'The Case' Case, Ferreira Rodrigues 'Dani' Daniel, Efan 'The Chief' Ekoku, Steve 'Fletch' Fletcher, Patrick 'Mike' Gilmore, Gordon 'Bob' Hardy, Eugene 'Mickey' Jones, Trevor 'Mop Head' Lee, Ted 'Super Mac' MacDougall, Billy 'Dossie' Miles, Paul 'Mozzy' Morrell, Mark 'Guppy' Morris, Mark 'Des' O'Connor, Sean 'Noisy' O'Driscoll, Emmanuel 'Manny' Omoyinmi, Harry 'Titch' Pearson, Francisco 'Frank' Peed, Roger 'Lou' Peters, Theo 'Tot' Pike, Lancelot 'Lance' Richardson, Kevin 'Rooster' Russell, Jimmy 'Chalky' White and Laurence 'Dai' Woodward. And of course many players have had the letter 'y' added to their surname, such as Kevin 'Bondy' and Jack 'Corky' plus 'Smithy' and 'Browny'. There have been quite a few Jocks and Paddys, also a 'Steino' and how can anyone ever forget a certain Irishman, George Best, who was universally known as 'Bestie' and 'El Beatle'.

CLEAN SHEETS

Up to the end of the 2014/15 season, Bournemouth had competed in a total of 3,828 Football League matches and, in more than 1,120 of them, their goalkeeper kept a clean sheet. Mark Overdale was quite superb in 1998/99. The shot-stopper kept his fort intact in 21 of Bournemouth's 46 league games. He also had 12 league shut-outs the following season. Iraq-born custodian Shwan Jalal was also in outstanding form in 2009/10, with 18 shut-outs. Jimmy Glass kept ten clean sheets for the Cherries (in 13 games) between 25 January and 1 April 1997. In fact, Glass did not concede a single goal in 13 games that season and he also stood firm in 1997/98, giving nothing away in 17 matches.Neil Moss also had 17 clean sheets for Bournemouth in 2003/04, while Lee Camp kept a clean sheet in four successive league matches in March 2014 for five in six games overall.

EXCELLENT CUP RUN

Bournemouth scored 20 goals and conceded only 11 in the seven FA Cup matches they played in 1928/29. The Cherries made progress by beating Poole Town (away) 4-1 and Guildford (also away) 5-1, before drawing 1-1 at Accrington Stanley. After winning the replay 2-0, they proceeded to knock out Watford 6-4 in a thrilling fourth round encounter at Dean Court and then held West Ham United 1-1 at home in round five, only to lose the replay 3-1 at Upton Park.

WHERE THE CHERRIES HAVE PLAYED THEIR FOOTBALL

This is a breakdown of Bournemouth's Football League status, 1923–2015 inclusive:

Seasons	Football League
1923–57	Third Division (South)
1957–70	Third Division
1970/71	Fourth Division
1971–75	Third Division
1975–82	Fourth Division
1982–87	Third Division
1987–90	Second Division
1990–92	Third Division
1992–2002	Second Division
2002/03	Third Division
2003/04	Second Division
2004–08	League 1
2008–10	League 2
2010–13	League 1
2013–15	Championship

And of course they earned the right to compete in the Premier League for the very first time in 2015/16.

BAD DAY AT THE OFFICE

Czech Republic youth international goalkeeper Marek Stech played in only one Football League game for Bournemouth, on loan from West Ham United, and what a nightmare he had. He deputised for Shwan Jalal against Morecambe at The Globe Arena in mid-December 2009 and had a real 'stinker'. The Cherries got smashed 5-0 (their worst defeat of the season) and poor old Stech walked off the pitch a sad, sad man.

OUSTED BY THE MINNOWS

Since gaining entry to the Third Division South in 1923, Bournemouth have been humiliated in the FA Cup by eight teams from outside the Football League. Here are those details of those eight cup disasters:

Season	Opponents	Venue	Score
1945/46	Lovells Athletic	Away	4-6*
1958/59	Tooting & Mitcham	Away	1-3
1961/62	Margate	Home	0-3
1970/71	Yeovil Town	Home	0-1
1974/75	Wycombe Wds.	Home	1-2
2002/03	Accrington Stanley	Away	3-5†
2005/06	Tamworth	Home	1-2
2008/09	Blyth Spartans	Away	0-1

* This was a two-legged tie which Lovells won on aggregate. † This game was decided on penalties.

BIG FA CUP REPLAY WINS

After drawing 1-1 with Caernarfon Town in an FA Cup second round tie in 1929/30, Bournemouth won the replay 5-2. Six seasons later, in the 1935/36 competition, the Cherries drew 1-1 at Walthamstow Avenue before hammering the non-leaguers 8-1 in the replay. A 0-0 draw at Dartford in 1937/38 was followed by an emphatic 6-0 win at Dean Court. In 1965/66, Bournemouth beat Weymouth 4-1 in a replay after a 0-0 draw a few miles along the Dorset coast. Oxford City held Bournemouth 1-1 in a first round tie in 1971/72 before crashing to an 8-1 defeat at Dean Court. In 1984/85, Bournemouth drew 1-1 at Dartford in a second round tie and then at Dean Court, the Cherries eased to a 4-1 win. Four years later a long journey north to Hartlepool resulted in a 1-1 draw, but it was all Bournemouth in the replay as 'Pool were defeated 5-2. In stark contrast, after holding Liverpool to a goalless draw at Dean Court in 1967/68, the Cherries lost the Anfield replay 4-1.

AFC ADDED TO NAME

AFC was added to Bournemouth under John Bond's reign as manager in 1972. However, this is only a trade name – as the club itself is still officially registered with the Football League and FA as Bournemouth and Boscombe Athletic Football Club.

CLUB BADGE

In 1972, Bournemouth adopted a new club badge as a symbol of their progress. There were stripes placed in the background, depicting the club's shirt, while in the foreground there was a player heading the ball, chosen in honour of ex-forward Dickie Dowsett, who was a prolific scorer for the club during the 1950s and 1960s.

PLACE NAMES

The following Bournemouth players were certainly not born in the place of their name: David Birmingham, Lewis Buxton, Jack Cork, Sam Dudley, Nick Fenton, Matt Holland, Pat Holland, Marcus Oldbury, Carl Preston and Jack Sutton. Here are a couple of coincidences: 1970s Cherries star Frank Barton was actually born in Barton-on-Humber in October 1947, while 1928/29 forward Sam Dudley was born in Tipton near Dudley, deep in the heart of the Black Country, in 1905.

BLESSED WITH ANOTHER JOB?

Cherries players who could have been mistaken if they had another job or pastime (spellings not taken into account): Dan Archer, Steve Baker, Ian Bishop, Richard Cadette, Billy Clark, Brian Clark, Colin Clarke, Steve Cook, Harry Cooke, Richard Cooke, Stephen Cooke, Shaun Cooper, Ian Cox, Reg Cutler, Harold Duke, Harry Falconer, Brian Farmer, Ernie King, John King, Andy Marshall, Joe Miller, Paul Miller, Ralph Miller, Marcos Painter, Brett Pitman, David Shearer, Jimmy Singer, Daryl Taylor, Lyle Taylor, Bob Walker and Robert Walker. And you have manager Freddie Cox as well.

INTO THE SECOND TIER

Harry Redknapp guided Bournemouth into the second tier of the Football League for the first time in their history as Third Division champions in 1987. After comfortably holding their own in their first season in a higher division, the Cherries made a stern and honest challenge at gaining promotion to the top flight in 1988/89. But unfortunately they fell away late in the season and eventually settled for a 12th place finish, which remained their highest-ever Football League placing until the 2013/14 season.

CHERRY CREATURES, POSSIBLY!

Here are four players, associated with Bournemouth, who were certainly not what their name suggests: Chris Ferrett, Alex Moth, Mark

Nightingale, Gavin Peacock, Theo 'Tot' Pike and Shaun Teale. And how about Jack Russell!

NINE-GOAL BONANZA

In October 2003, a crowd of 6,388 at Dean Court saw a nine-goal thriller between Bournemouth and Luton Town in the Third Division. Steve Fletcher put the Cherries ahead on seven minutes and after that it was action at both ends of the field, with the goals flying in as follows: A Stephen Purches own goal on ten minutes (1-1); Hughes for Luton on 25 minutes (1-2); Brian Stock for the Cherries, 34 minutes (2-2); Gareth O'Connor, 42 minutes (3-2 to Bournemouth); Fletcher again, right on half-time (4-2); Adrian Forbes on the hour for Luton (4-3); Stock, again 62 minutes (5-3) and finally Wade Elliott 67 minutes (6-3). Late on, both James Hayter and Elliott missed easy chances for the Cherries, likewise Kevin Foley and Lee Mansell for the Hatters.

5-3 DEFEATS

Bournemouth succumbed to two 5-3 league defeats in 1997/98 – going down in eight-goal thrillers at Bristol Rovers in late December and at Southend United in March. All six Cherries goals were scored by different players.

LAST-DAY TROUBLE AND RELEGATION

On 5 May 1990 – the final day of the league season – Leeds United visited Dean Court, knowing they had to beat Bournemouth to stand a chance of winning the Second Division championship and so gain promotion to the First Division. It was a quite a day all round. Some visiting supporters caused trouble in the town during the morning of the game and the atmosphere inside the ground was tense to say the least. As it was Leeds won the game 1-0 and, combined with the results of other matches, meant they were promoted while sadly Bournemouth were relegated. The violence and destruction by visitors to Bournemouth continued over the holiday weekend, causing more than £1m of damage, and injury to fans and police officers. The *Daily Echo* newspaper reported, 'Spectators, including many young children, had to run to safety as missiles were hurled and riot police waded in to control the crowds.' The matter was later raised in Parliament by one of the town's MPs. Financially, the Leeds trouble affected the club for more than a decade, as Bournemouth were prevented by local police from staging home games on Bank Holidays (traditionally a popular day for football) for thirteen years, until Shrewsbury Town came to town on 21 April 2003.

HONOURS

Here is a list of honours won by the Cherries:
• Championship: Winners 2014/15
• Third Division: Winners 1986/87
• League 1: Runners-up 2012/13
• League 2: Runners-up 2009/10
• Fourth Division: Runners-up 1970/71
• Third Division: Play-off winners 2002/03
• Third Division South: Runners-up 1947/48
• Football League Associate Members Cup: Winners 1983/84
• Football League Third Division South Cup: Winners 1945/46
• Southern League: Runners-up 1922/23

NO CUP EXEMPTION

When Bournemouth were elected to the Football League in 1923 they were not given exemption from the qualifying rounds of the FA Cup. As a result they were drawn to play the Portesca Gas Company team in a preliminary round but, after discussions, the Cherries refused to fulfil the fixture and withdrew from the competition.

I'M IN CHARGE

There have been 31 official team managers of Bournemouth since the club first entered the Southern League in 1914. And they are:

Name	Dates
Vincent Kitcher*	1914–23
Harry Kinghorn	1923–25
Leslie Knighton	1925–28
Frank Richards*	1928–30
Billy Birrell	1930–35
Bob Crompton	1935/36
Charlie Bell	1936–39
Harry Kinghorn	1939–47
Harry Lowe	1947–50
Jack Bruton	1950–56
Freddie Cox	1956–58
Don Welsh	1958–61
Bill McGarry	1961–63
Reg Flewin	1963–65
Freddie Cox	1965–70
John Bond	1970–73
Trevor Hartley	1974/75

John Benson............................ 1975–78
Alec Stock............................... 1979/80
David Webb........................... 1980–82
Don Megson 1983
Harry Redknapp.................... 1983–92
Tony Pulis 1992–94
Mel Machin 1994–2000
Sean O'Driscoll 2000–06
Kevin Bond 2006-08
Jimmy Quinn 2008
Eddie Howe........................... 2008–11
Lee Bradbury 2011/12
Paul Groves................................ 2012
Eddie Howe..................... 2012 to date

* Served as secretary-manager.

MANAGERIAL NOTEPAD

Vincent Kitcher, a local businessman, looked after the team's fortunes for nine years, August 1914 to May 1923. He did the spadework and paperwork ahead of the club's election to the Football League at the AGM in the summer of 1923.

Harry Kinghorn, a Scot born in Midlothian in 1886, kept goal for Alloa Athletic and Leith, and made 25 League appearances for Sheffield Wednesday from 1908 to 1911. After World War One, he became Bournemouth's assistant boss (July 1920) before taking over as manager three years later. In 1925 he stepped down to take over as the club's first team trainer, a position he held for 14 years, up to the outbreak of World War Two, when he started a second spell as boss at Dean Court which lasted for another eight years. Kinghorn was associated with Bournemouth Football Club for over half a century, making him one of the club's longest serving members. In 1928/29, he came out of retirement to play on the left wing at the age of 42. In charge of the Cherries when they won the Third Division South Cup in 1946, he was manager for 131 games, winning 45, drawing 27 and losing 59.

Frank Richards, when engaged as secretary-manager of Birmingham, failed to submit the entry form to allow the Midland club to play in the 1921/22 FA Cup competition. A Brummie, born in 1880, he had two spells with the Blues, firstly as an office clerk and secretary-manager from 1906–25, leading the club to promotion as Second Division champions in 1921, and then as manager in season 1927/28. In between times he was in charge of Preston North End. He then bossed Bournemouth for three seasons, during which time the Cherries reached the fifth round of the FA Cup. He died in 1963.

Leslie Knighton also managed Birmingham, from 1928–33. Born near Burton-on-Trent in 1884, he played for Burton United before taking over as boss of Castleford Town in 1904, switching to Huddersfield as assistant secretary-manager in 1909. A strict disciplinarian, he held a similar position with Manchester City from 1912 to 1919 and was in charge of Arsenal for six years (1919–25) before taking over at Bournemouth. On leaving Dean Court in 1928, he returned to St Andrews for a second spell, and later managed Chelsea (1933–39) and Shrewsbury (1945–48). He retired to Dorset and became secretary of a local golf club, while also managing Portishead FC (1952–53). Knighton died in Bournemouth in May 1959, after a short illness.

Billy Birrell, born in Scotland in 1897, was a forward with Raith Rovers and Middlesbrough, scoring 59 goals in 225 league appearances for the latter. After retiring he took up management, first with Bournemouth (appointed in May 1930), then with Queens Park Rangers (April 1935–May 1939) and finally with Chelsea (May 1939–May 1952). He twice took the latter club to the semi-finals of the FA Cup (1950 and 1952). He later worked as a clerk in Kenton, London, and died in November 1968.

Bob Crompton, a superb full-back, won 41 caps for England and made 576 appearances for Blackburn Rovers between 1896 and 1920, captaining the team to First Division titles in 1912 and 1914. Born in Blackburn in 1879, he played for the local Trinity club before signing as a professional for Rovers. During World War One Crompton guested for Blackpool and, after retiring, served as a director at Ewood Park. He was appointed Rovers manager in December 1926, holding office until February 1931. He spent only eight months in charge of Bournemouth, returning home to Blackburn, and acting as honorary manager from April 1938 until his death in March 1941.

Charlie Bell, born in Scotland in 1884, played centre-forward for Carlisle City, Woolwich Arsenal (for whom he scored twice in his only league game v. Leicester in December 1913), Chesterfield, Barrow (top scorer in 1920/21) and Queens Park Rangers. Attaining the rank of captain in the Footballers' Battalion of the Middlesex Regiment during WW1, he retired as a footballer in 1922 to become trainer of Reading. He was Notts County's spongeman in 1922/23 and managed Wigan Borough in 1923/24 before leaving the game for ten years. He returned as Mansfield Town's trainer in July 1934 and served as their manager the following year before taking over at Bournemouth in February 1936. He remained at Dean Court until May 1939 and, after the War, moved abroad, coaching in Italy, Portugal, Brazil and France. Bell died in Scotland in 1956.

Harry Lowe was born in Cheshire in 1886 and was a centre-half with Brighton & Hove Albion, Tottenham Hotspur and Fulham before taking over as Spurs' coach in 1932. He then went into management in 1935, taking charge of Deportivo Espanyol in Spain. He bossed Bournemouth for three seasons in the late 1940s, guiding the Cherries to second place in League Division Three (S) in 1948, four points behind QPR. Later in charge of Yeovil (1951-53), he died in London in 1966.

Jack Bruton, born in Westhoughton, Lancashire in 1903, played outside-right for Wigan Borough, Burnley and Blackburn Rovers before retiring during World War Two after scoring 104 goals in 304 appearances for the latter club. He also won three England caps and twice represented the Football League. After serving as assistant-secretary at Ewood Park, he then managed Rovers before taking over at Bournemouth in March 1950, holding office for six years. Appointed as trainer-coach at Dean Court, he remained at the club until May 1960. Later engaged as coach and scout by Portsmouth, Bruton also scouted for his former club, Blackburn. He died in Bournemouth in March 1986.

Don Welsh played in three full and nine World War Two internationals for England and made over 200 appearances for Charlton Athletic with whom he won the FA Cup in 1947 as captain, having been a loser 12 months earlier. He also gained a Third Division South championship medal in 1935 and a War League (S) Cup winner's medal in 1944 with the Addicks. Born in Manchester in 1911, he served in the Royal Navy before becoming a footballer with Torquay United in 1934. From Plainmoor he switched to Charlton (1935) and remained at The Valley until retiring in 1947. He also guested for Valetta (Malta), Southend, Aldershot, Brighton & Hove Albion, Chester, Liverpool, Manchester City and Millwall during the hostilities. Manager of Brighton (1947-51) and Liverpool (1951-56), he then ran a pub in Devon before returning to management with Bournemouth in July 1958, remaining at Dean Court until February 1961. After that Welsh took over Clubland Cumberwell Youth Club Centre and managed Wycombe Wanderers (1963/64) before ending his footballing days in the offices of Charlton. He died in Stevenage in 1990.

Bill McGarry, a wing-half born in Stoke-on-Trent in 1927, played for Port Vale (1945–51) and Huddersfield (1951–61) before serving as Bournemouth's player-manager from March 1961 until May 1963 when he took a similar position with Watford. McGarry then managed Ipswich Town (1964–68), Wolves (1968–76), the Saudi Arabia national team (1976/77) and Newcastle (1977–80), scouted for Brighton, coached FC Power Dynamo in Zambia and also the Zambian national team before returning to Molineux for a second spell as manager in 1985. He ended his footballing life in Bophuthatswana in 1994. McGarry made 146 league appearances for Port Vale, 363 for Huddersfield and 78 for the Cherries. He won the Second Division title with Ipswich in 1968, and guided Wolves to the UEFA Cup Final in 1972 and League Cup glory in 1974, won four England caps and toured South Africa with the FA in the 1950s. He died in South Africa in 2005.

Freddie Cox, an outside-right with Tottenham Hotspur, Arsenal and West Bromwich Albion, scored 25 goals in 182 league games during his career from 1938–54, gaining an FA Cup winner's medal with the Gunners in 1950. Born in Reading in 1920, Cox joined Spurs from Northfleet and during World War Two guested with Fulham, Manchester City, Reading and Swindon Town. He was player-coach at WBA under former manager Vic Buckingham. In April 1956 Cox took over the reins at Dean Court and as every Cherries supporter knows, he did extraordinary well (especially in the FA Cup) before leaving in July 1958 to take charge of Portsmouth. He later had a three-year spell as manager of Gillingham, leading the Kent club to the Fourth Division title in 1964. He served Bournemouth for a second time from April 1965 until June 1970 when he quit football to run a newsagents business in Bournemouth, the town where he died in 1973.

Reg Flewin was a First Division champion with Portsmouth in 1949 and 1950, toured Canada and Australia with the FA, and played in one Wartime international for England. Born in Portsmouth in 1920, he made 167 appearances at centre-half for Pompey in 16 years, 1937–53. After retiring he became trainer-coach at Fratton Park and also served as assistant manager. He bossed Stockport County (1960–63) before spending two seasons in charge of Bournemouth. On retiring Flewin settled on the Isle of Wight, where he managed the Fort Warden holiday camp in Totland Bay. He died in Shanklin in 2008, aged 87, a week after Portsmouth had beaten Cardiff City 1-0 in the FA Cup Final.

John Bond was another FA Cup winner, helping West Ham beat Preston 3-2 in the 1964 final. A full-back, he also helped the Hammers win the Second Division title in 1958, represented the Football League and toured South Africa with the FA in 1956. Born in Colchester in 1932, Bond spent 17 years at Upton Park (1949–66), making 428 appearances. He then played for Torquay United before retiring in 1969 to become coach of Gillingham. Appointed Bournemouth manager in May 1970, he quickly transformed the club and guided the Cherries into the Third Division in his first season. He almost achieved promotion again the following term, but missed out on the last game of the campaign. He left Dean Court in November 1973 to take over at Norwich City and when he left Dean Court (with his aide Ken Brown) in 1973, the Cherries received £10,000 in compensation. Later boss of Manchester City, Burnley, Swansea City, Birmingham City, Shrewsbury Town and Witton Albion, he quit football in 1999, having gained promotion to the First Division and reached the League Cup Final with Norwich, and lost in the 1981 FA Cup Final with Manchester City. Bond's son, Kevin, took over as Bournemouth manager in 2006; six years later his father died.

Trevor Hartley, born in Doncaster in 1947, was an inside-forward with West Ham (1964–69) and Bournemouth (1969–71). On retiring he became coach at Dean Court, moving up to manager in November 1973. In January 1975 he was replaced in the hotseat by John Benson, but remained in football as director of coaching in Singapore before returning to the UK to become Luton Town's reserve team coach (1984/85). Later engaged as assistant manager and caretaker manager at Tottenham Hotspur (1986–88), he spent two more years coaching in Malaysia before leaving football in 1990.

John Benson, born in Arbroath, Scotland in 1942, was a defender with Manchester City (1961–64), Torquay United (1964–70), Bournemouth (1970–73), Exeter City (on loan), Norwich City (1973–75) and Bournemouth again (as player-manager, 1975–79). He then returned to Manchester City, initially as assistant manager (October 1980), then served as manager (for four months in 1983), bossed Burnley (1984/85) and acted as Barnsley's chief scout in the 1990s. He spent most of his career following John Bond around the football circuit, playing with him at Torquay, under him at Dean Court and Carrow Road, and as his senior coach at Maine Road. During his career Benson made 469 appearances. He won promotion with Exeter in 1966 and with Bournemouth in 1971, but was unable to get the Cherries out of the Fourth Division as manager. He took over from Bond as manager at Maine Road and also at Burnley.

Alec Stock, born in Somerset in 1917, was a pre-World War Two forward with Tottenham Hotspur (amateur), Charlton Athletic and QPR (1935–39). He took over as player-manager of Yeovil Town in 1946 and led the Glovers to a famous 2-1 FA Cup victory over Sunderland three years later. He later had three spells in charge of Leyton Orient, bossed AS Roma, QPR, Luton Town and Fulham as well as Bournemouth (1979/80), after which he served as general manager of Dean Court until 1981 and a club director for five years, up to 1986.

David Webb scored a dramatic winning goal for Chelsea against Leeds in the 1970 FA Cup Final replay at Old Trafford and the following year helped the Londoners beat Real Madrid in the European Cup Winners' Cup Final. As a defender, he made almost 600 club appearances while also serving with Leyton Orient, Southampton, QPR, Leicester City, Derby County, Bournemouth (as player-coach from May 1980) and Torquay United. He was Cherries manager from December 1980 until February 1982 when he was sacked after a dispute with the chairman over new ownership of the club. Webb was later in charge of Southend United, his former club Chelsea and Brentford.

Don Megson made over 450 appearances as a full-back with Sheffield Wednesday (1953–70), Portland Timbers (player-coach) and Bristol Rovers (player-manager). He took over the reins at Dean Court from Webb but lasted only seven months, losing his job after the Cherries had crashed to a record 9-0 League defeat at Lincoln. An FA Cup winner with the Owls in 1966, his son Gary Megson also played for and managed Sheffield Wednesday.

Harry Redknapp was appointed caretaker boss of the Cherries in December 1982 – just after that debacle at Sincil Bank. Born in Poplar, London in 1947, winger Redknapp scored 14 goals in 316 appearances playing for West Ham (1964–72), Bournemouth (1972–74), Phoenix Fire in the NASL, Brentford and Seattle Sounders in the NASL. After acting as assistant manager at Oxford City, he was appointed player-coach at Dean Court in October 1982, taking over as manager a year later. After leaving Bournemouth he returned to West Ham as assistant boss before later managing the Hammers, as well as Tottenham Hotspur, Southampton, Portsmouth, Crystal Palace and QPR. He won the Associate Members Cup (1984) and the Third Division title (1987) as Cherries manager, and guided West Ham to InterToto glory in 1999, Portsmouth to the First Division title and FA Cup glory in 2003 and 2008 respectively, and led QPR into the Premier League in 2014. This was his managerial record with the Cherries: played 457, won 180, drawn 107, and lost 170. Overall, Redknapp was a club manager for 1,380 matches, winning 556, drawing 344 and losing 480. His son Jamie Redknapp, married to pop star Louise Nurding, starred in over 350 games as a midfielder for Bournemouth (1989–91), Liverpool, Tottenham Hotspur and Southampton, as well as gaining one B, 18 Under-21 and 17 full caps for England.

Tony Pulis, of Maltese extraction, was born in Pillwenlly, near Newport, South Wales in 1958. A defender, he won Welsh Youth caps and played for Bristol Rovers (two spells), Happy Valley in Hong Kong, Newport County, Bournemouth (July 1986 to May 1989), Gillingham and Bournemouth again (as player-manager, June 1992–94), making 373 club appearances. Leaving Dean Court, he became manager of Gillingham, then Bristol City, Portsmouth, Stoke City, Plymouth Argyle, Stoke (again), Crystal Palace and West Bromwich Albion. As a player, he gained a Third Division championship medal with Bournemouth in 1987 and, as a manager, guided Stoke to the 2011 FA Cup Final and kept both Crystal Palace and West Bromwich Albion in the Premier League. Pulis's record as Cherries manager was: played 107, won 31, drawn 38 and lost 38. His brother Ray played for Newport, while his father-in-law, Bill Stroud, starred for Southampton, Leyton Orient and also Newport.

Mel Machin, born in Newcastle-under-Lyme in 1945, was a midfielder with Port Vale, Gillingham, Bournemouth (1970–73), Norwich City and Seattle Sounders (NASL). He retired in 1977 with almost 450 club appearances to his name and went on to manage Manchester City (1987–89) and Barnsley before returning to Dean Court as boss of the Cherries in September 1994. In August 2000, he moved upstairs as the club's director of football, before having a spell as caretaker boss of Huddersfield Town. Machin's record as Cherries' manager was: played 322, won 119, drawn 121 and lost 82.

Sean O'Driscoll, born in Wolverhampton in 1957, was a midfielder with Fulham (1979–84) and Bournemouth (1984–95). He also won three caps for the Republic of Ireland and, when he took off his boots in 1995, he had made a record 423 league appearances for the Cherries, a feat since beaten by Steve Fletcher. On retiring, O'Driscoll joined the club's coaching staff and, in August 2000, was appointed manager. However, despite limited financial resources, he achieved some good results, including promotion from the Third Division in 2002/03. He left his position in September 2006 season, and in later years managed Doncaster Rovers, Crawley Town, Nottingham Forest, Bristol City and also the England Under-19 team.

Kevin Bond, born in West Ham in 1957, was a youth team player with Bournemouth when his father was manager in 1973. He was released by the club in 1974 and signed for Norwich City, later playing for Seattle Sounders (NASL), Manchester City and Southampton before returning to Dean Court in 1988 and staying this time for four years. He then assisted Exeter City, Sittingbourne and Dover Athletic before retiring in 1996. Capped twice by England B, he made over 600 appearances (537 in the Football League; 126 for the Cherries) and played 100 or more games for four different clubs, serving alongside Harry Redknapp many times. After spells as a coach with Manchester City, Wrexham and Altrincham, Bond managed Stafford Rangers (1997/98) before having various coaching and scouting roles with Portsmouth (two spells), West Ham and Newcastle. He became Bournemouth boss in mid-October 2006, signing a short-term contract until the end of the season. Although the Cherries lost the first five games of his reign, they avoided relegation and Bond was awarded a new contract. Unfortunately a ten-point deduction for entering administration saw the club relegated to League 2 at the end of 2007/08, in spite of a run of five wins in the last six games. Bournemouth then had a further 17 points deducted for the 2008/09 season and, after a dismal start to that campaign, Bond and his management team of Rob Newman and Eddie Howe were dismissed, the Cherries having picked up just two points from the first four matches. A month later, Bond was reunited with Redknapp as assistant manager of Tottenham and then followed him to QPR. In September 2006, the FA officially announced that it was to investigate allegations 'relating to players' agents and connected activities' concerning Bond, following a BBC *Panorama* special on corruption in football. Newcastle placed Bond on 'gardening leave' soon after the broadcast, and subsequently terminated his contract, replacing him with Sam Allardyce. Ironically, Allardyce was also accused of accepting illegal payments in the same *Panorama* programme.

Jimmy Quinn, born in Belfast in 1959, had a career spanning 22 years from 1976–98. A prolific goalscorer, the pinnacle of his footballing days was winning the Second Division Golden Boot award for 1993/94 when he netted 40 goals for Reading, who were promoted as champions. Quinn played for Whitchurch Alport, Congleton Town, Oswestry, Swindon Town (three spells), Blackburn Rovers, Leicester City, Bradford City, West Ham, Bournemouth, Reading, Peterborough, Northwich Victoria (two spells), Hereford, Highworth Town, Hayes, Shrewsbury Town and lastly Nantwich Town. He netted over 250 goals in more than 750 club and international appearances, including 214 in 595 league games, 19 in 43 outings for the Cherries in 1991/92. He also struck 12 goals in 46 games for Northern Ireland (1985–96). Moving into management, first with Reading in 1994, Quinn went on to boss his former clubs Swindon, Northwich Victoria, Shrewsbury and then Bournemouth. He was in charge of Bournemouth for 121 days from September to December 2008 before being sacked after a run of poor results, including a 2-0 home defeat to fellow relegation battlers Barnet. He then bossed Nantwich, Egersund IK (Norway) and Cambridge United, and overall was associated with 20 clubs as a player and manager.

Eddie Howe began his career with Bournemouth in 1994, having played locally for Parley Sports and Rossgarth YFC. Making his league debut against Hull City, he soon established himself in the side, his displays earning him many admirers. Selected in the Football League side against Italy's Serie B team in a friendly, he was also capped by England at Under-21 level in the Toulon Tournament in 1998. In March 2002, after 237 appearances for the Cherries, Howe moved to Portsmouth for £400,000 – Harry Redknapp's first signing as Pompey manager. However, shortly after his transfer, a knee injury suffered on his debut against Preston ended his season. He returned at the start of 2002/03 against Nottingham Forest, but was injured again after just nine minutes and was ruled out for another entire campaign. Finally regaining full fitness, after 18 months out, he was loaned to Swindon Town in March 2004. Portsmouth then loaned Howe back to Bournemouth for the first three months of the next season and, after proving his fitness, he was re-signed permanently by the Cherries in November 2004 after chairman Peter Phillips had made an appeal over the internet for fans to pledge money to buy Howe. Indeed, such was Howe's popularity at Dean Court, the club received pledges of £13,500 in less than two days. In December 2006, aged 29, Howe was appointed player-coach by manager Kevin Bond. Asked to look after the second team, he still continued to play in the senior side. He eventually retired in May 2007 (after the knee injury flared up again), but in September 2008, Howe lost his job along with Bond. As keen as ever, Howe returned to Dean Court as a youth coach under new boss Jimmy Quinn and took over as caretaker manager when Quinn was sacked on New Year's Eve 2008. Even though his two games in charge ended in away defeats, he was given the position as the Cherries' full-time manager in mid-January 2009. And what a great job he did, guiding the club out of the relegation zone despite a 17-point deficit. At the start of the 2009/10 campaign, Bournemouth won eight out of nine games, a club record, but in the November, Championship club Peterborough United approached Howe to replace Darren Ferguson as their manager. Howe rejected Posh's overtures. Despite the club's transfer embargo remaining in place for the rest of the season, The Cherries, under Howe's astute guidance, gained promotion to League 1 after two years in the fourth tier of English football thanks to a 2-0 win at Burton Albion on 24 April 2010. However, early in January 2011, Howe, having already been approached by several clubs, surprisingly left Bournemouth to take over as manager of Burnley. He took charge of his 102nd Cherries match on the same day he signed a three-and-a-half year contract at Turf Moor. Sadly, it ended in a 2-1 defeat at Colchester. On 12 October 2012, Howe left Burnley and rejoined Bournemouth. He quickly won the League 1 Manager of the Month award for November after guiding the club to three wins and two draws, as well as an FA Cup victory over Dagenham & Redbridge. He then set about moving the Cherries up the ladder, and what a terrific job he did. As the promotion race began to hot up, the team hit top form, producing a run of eight successive wins, starting in mid-March and culminating with a 3-1 home victory over Carlisle in April which sealed promotion to the Championship. Things got better and better and, in 2013/14, the Cherries finished tenth in the Championship (only six points off the play-offs), and then, in 2014/15, it all happened with promotion to the Premier League being gained. Howe's record as Bournemouth's manager (two spells) up to the final game of the

2014/15 season makes pretty impressive reading: played 244, won 127, drawn 49 and lost 68. He won exactly half of the 102 games he was in charge of during his first spell and 76 out of 142 in his second. To crown a marvellous 2014/15 season, he was named Football League Manager of the Decade at the annual Football League Awards ceremony, having earlier won the Championship Manager of the Month award for October, December and March, following up with the Championship Manager of the Season award. And for those interested, Howe was a boyhood Everton supporter and Gary Lineker was his hero.

Lee Bradbury, born in Cowes on the Isle of Wight in 1975, was a striker and then full-back. He played for 11 different clubs between 1995 and 2011, scoring 92 goals in 512 league games, including ten in 127 outings for Bournemouth in four seasons from August 2007. He started his career with Portsmouth and, after assisting Exeter City, Manchester City, Crystal Palace, Birmingham City, Portsmouth (again), Sheffield Wednesday, Derby County, Walsall, Oxford United and Southend United, he moved to Dean Court, initially on loan. He was appointed player/caretaker manager by the Cherries in January 2011 when Howe moved north to Burnley, and was given the job full-time 13 days later. He did well, leading the team into the play-offs that season, only for the Cherries to lose on penalties to Huddersfield in the two-legged semi-final. Unfortunately a run of poor results led to Bradbury's sacking in January 2012, allowing Paul Groves to step into his place before Howe returned in October 2012.

Paul Groves, a hard-working midfielder, scored 104 goals in 669 league appearances in seventeen years from 1988 to 2005 (he played over 800 games in all). Born in Derby in 1966, he began with Belper Town and, after starring for Burton Albion, entered the Football League with Leicester City. He went on to play for Lincoln City, Blackpool, Grimsby Town (two spells), West Bromwich Albion (signed for £600,000 in 1996), Scunthorpe United, York City and Stafford Rangers, retiring in 2006. Player-manager of Grimsby for three seasons (2001–04), he was caretaker manager of Portsmouth in 2009 – after three years on the Fratton Park coaching staff, and, in July 2010, joined West Ham as senior coach. A year later he became youth coach at Bournemouth and, in March 2012, following Bradbury's departure, was given the role as caretaker manager. He had 20 games in charge (three won, 11 drawn and six lost) before Howe returned for his second spell in charge. Groves left the Cherries in January 2014 and five months later became first team coach at Crawley Town. He won the Football League Trophy with Grimsby in 1998… albeit at Bournemouth's expense.

ASSISTANT BOSSES

Most managers usually engage an assistant (or head coach) and here are a few of the men who have worked for the Cherries in this capacity over the last 45 years or so: Reg Tyrrell (1970s); Jimmy Gabriel, Stuart Morgan, Terry Shanahan and Keith Williams (1980s); Roger Brown, Mike Trusson, David Williams and John Williams (1990s); Peter Grant, Rob Newman, Richard O'Kelly and Joe Roach (2000s) followed by Shaun Brookes, Steve Fletcher and Jason Tindall in recent years.

HAT-TRICK HEROES

On 24 February 2004, Bournemouth striker James Hayter scored the fastest hat-trick in Football League history. Coming on as an 84th-minute substitute, he netted three times in just two minutes and 17 seconds against Wrexham in a Second Division game at Dean Court. The Cherries won 6-0 in front of 5,899 spectators. Hayter also scored a six-minute hat-trick in his four-timer in Bournemouth's 5-2 win over Bury at Gigg Lane in October 2000. His treble came in the 55th, 60th and 61st minutes. Two players – Marc Pugh in the 8-0 win at Birmingham and Brett Pitman in the 4-0 home victory over Blackpool – scored hat-tricks for the Cherries in 2014/15. And, in August 2015, Callum Wilson became the first Bournemouth player to score three goals in a Premier League game when the Cherries won 4-3 at West Ham.

SHARE AND SHARE ALIKE

No less than 26 players scored at least one goal for Bournemouth in 2011/12. They were Addison, Arter, Barrett, Cooper, Daniels, Feeney, S. Fletcher, Fogden, Gregory, Hines, Lovell, Macdonald, McDermott, Malone, Pugh, Purches, Sheringham, Stockley, Symes, Taylor, Thomas, Tubbs and Zubar, plus opponents Duffy (Exeter), Frampton (Gillingham) and Ngala (Yeovil Town). Bournemouth had 20 different goalscorers (including opponents) in 2002/03 and 2008/09, and 19 in 2006/07 and 18 in 2004/05, 2007/08, 2010/11 and 2012/13.

GREAT GESTURE

Bournemouth supporters raised almost £3,000 to help Burton Albion fans travel to their re-arranged FA Cup tie in January 2014. The original game was called off an hour before kick-off due to the Cherries' Goldsands Stadium pitch being waterlogged. And the late postponement meant around 200 ardent Burton followers made a fruitless 300-mile round trip to the south coast. Bournemouth fan and initiative organiser

David Whitehead told BBC Radio Solent, 'It shows there is another side to football.' Whitehead set up the fundraising page after recalling the generosity shown by several Burton supporters when Cherries fans celebrated promotion from League 2 at the Staffordshire club's Pirelli Stadium in 2010. 'They were so hospitable that day that there's been a special feeling between the clubs ever since,' he said. The money raised – £2,930 – was more than three times the original target of £800. Bournemouth chairman Jeff Mostyn said at the time, 'It's just the most incredible gesture and I think it's probably unprecedented in football for supporters to be so generous. On that day when we were promoted, after years of grief and struggling, for Ben Robinson, Burton chairman and all of his staff, the groundsmen and the stewards, to let us have the run of the ground was something that was incredible. Stewards by their very nature are designed to hold crowds at bay, but they were joining in the celebrations as well, and our supporters have never forgotten it.'

SAINTS LINK

Over the years, many in fact, scores of footballers and soccer men in general, have been associated with both Bournemouth and Southampton, and they include the following:

Ian Andrews (1990s), David Armstrong (1981–87), Stephen Baker (1978–91), Lee Barnard (2009–13), Vince Bartram (Cherries goalkeeper 1991–94, Saints coach 2013–15), Brian Bedford (1950s), Alan Blayney (2000–04), Kevin Bond (1974–82, also Cherries coach and manager), Phil Boyer (1970–77), Len Butt (1912––22), Jimmy Case (1985–91), Colin Clarke (1980s), Jack Cork (2006–14), James Coutts (ex-Saints junior, 2003–07), Martin Crainie (2003–05), Kevin Dawtry (1974–81), Dickie Dowsett (1950s, later Bournemouth commercial manager from 1968–83), Jack Fletcher (1930s), John Flood (1949–58), Tony Funnell (1977–81), Len Gaynor (1950s), Charlie George (1978––82), Simon Gillett (2003–09), Ivan Golac (1978––82), Jack Gregory (1943–59), John Hold (Saints trialist, 1960s), Ernie King (1920s), Phil Kite (1980s), Adam Lallana (2005–14), George Lawrence (1979–90), Herbert Lock (1920s), Charlie McDonagh (1930s), Jack McDonald (1940s/50s – scored 35 goals in 80 league games for Bournemouth), Scott McDonald (1999–2003), Ted MacDougall (1969–78), Doug McGibbon (1938––51, scorer of 65 goals in 103 league games for the Cherries), David McGoldrick (2005–09), Martin McGrath (1977–81), Neil Moss (1990s), Fred Perrett (1930s), Forbes Phillips-Masterson (1970s), David Puckett (1977–86), Harry Redknapp (Cherries player, also coach 1982/83; Saints manager 2004/05), Jamie Redknapp (1989–2005), Derek Reeves (1954–62), Dani/ Ferreira Rodrigues Daniel (1998–2005), Danny Seabourne (2009–13), Tony Sealy (1970s), Albert Shelley (1930s), Andrew Surman (2003–15),

Wayne Talkes (1967–75), Paul Telfer (2001–08), Jo Tessem (1999–2008), Jake Thomson (2006–09), Isaac Tomlinson (1900s, later Bournemouth scout), Chris Warren (1990s), David Webb (1980–84, Cherries player and manager 1980–82; Saints player 1966–68), Len Wheeler (1911–21), Bobby Whitelaw (1930s), Charlie Wilkinson (1930s) and Mark Whitlock (1977–88, made over 100 appearances for the Cherries). Isaac Tomlinson played for Southampton (1905–06) and later worked as a scout for Bournemouth (1929–32), while Dean Mooney played for Bournemouth (1980–84) and also starred for R.S. Southampton. Among the wartime guests who played for one or both clubs (1939–46), we have David Bewley, John McDonald, George Rothery, Charlie Wilkinson and Bob Young.

BEFORE AND AFTER A BREAK!

Bournemouth were outfoxed, outmanoeuvred and completely outplayed by Northampton Town for the first 45 minutes of their League game at the County Ground in March 1976. The Cobblers went in at the break leading 6-0 with centre-forward Jim Hall having bagged a hat-trick. The second half was more even, goalless in fact, with 6-0 the final result. Six goals were also scored during the first half of the Bournemouth v. Bristol Rovers Third Division South game in December 1927, three by each side. After the break the Cherries scored again to win the match 4-3. After a goalless first half, Bournemouth went for broke against 19th-placed Burnley at Dean Court in a Second Division game in November 1998, ending up 5-0 winners with goals from Christer Warren (55 minutes), Steve Robinson (a penalty on 60, and his second 69) and two from South African-born striker Mark Stein (74 and 89).

CHERRIES' HOME CROWDS

Details of the Cherries' average home league attendances, 1946/47 to 2014/15 inclusive:

1946/47	10,401
1947/48	16,854
1948/49	15,975
1949/50	14,559
1950/51	12,730
1951/52	10,968
1952/53	10,766
1953/54	9,727
1954/55	9,809
1955/56	8,035
1956/57	10,968
1957/58	12,624

1958/59	10,680
1959/60	10,403
1960/61	7,811
1961/62	11,622
1962/63	9,763
1963/64	9,830
1964/65	7,748
1965/66	6,329
1966/67	7,940
1967/68	5,983
1968/69	7,564
1969/70	5,401
1970/71	8,339
1971/72	12,990
1972/73	12,268
1973/74	8,981
1974/75	5,987
1975/76	4,460
1976/77	4,035
1977/78	3,343
1978/79	3,759
1979/80	3,924
1980/81	3,380
1981/82	5,933
1982/83	5,723
1983/84	4,035
1984/85	3,766
1985/86	3,423
1986/87	6,610
1987/88	7,873
1988/89	8,807
1989/90	7,454
1990/91	6,017
1991/92	5,471
1992/93	4,454
1993/94	4,355
1994/95	4,391
1995/96	4,213
1996/97	4,581
1997/98	4,732
1998/99	7,117
1999/2000	4,917
2000/01	4,403
2001/02	5,062

2002/03	5,829
2003/04	6,913
2004/05	7,123
2005/06	6,458
2006/07	6,028
2007/08	5,504
2008/09	4,931
2009/10	5,719
2010/11	7,103
2011/12	5,881
2012/13	6,852
2013/14	9,952
2014/15	10,307

ATTENDANCE FACTS

Only four times since 1950 has the average attendance at Bournemouth's home league games topped the 12,000 mark; only twice since 1973 has it topped 10,000, and, in fact, between 1974 and 1988, it didn't rise above 8,000.

The 3,433 average in 1977/78 has been Bournemouth's lowest since the World War Two. And prior to World War Two, the lowest average seasonal league attendance at Dean Court was 4,125 in 1925/26.

Between 1923 and 1939, Bournemouth's average home league attendance was 9,950; during the decade from 1946 to 1956 it was almost 12,000; it dropped to 9,778 for the ten-year period from 1965–75 and reduced by another 1,800 to 7,992 for the 1966–76 decade. The average over the last 40 seasons or so is around 6,000.

The biggest crowd for a competitive game at Dean Court was 28,799 for the Bournemouth v. Manchester United FA Cup sixth round tie in March 1957.

The best league crowd at Dean Court was 25,495 v. Queens Park Rangers in April 1948. In contrast, the lowest was 1,873 v. Lincoln City in March 1986. And only 2,203 fans attended the home league clash with York City in mid-November 1980.

A then-record crowd of 48,110 attended the Aston Villa v. Bournemouth Third Division game at Villa Park in February 1972. The Cherries lost 2-1.

Only 1,923 dedicated supporters saw Bournemouth lose 4-3 to Wolverhampton Wanderers in a Freight Rover Trophy game at Molineux in December 1986.

GROUND CAPACITY

This is how Bournemouth's home ground capacity has been reduced since the club's record attendance was set at Dean Court in 1957:

Seasons	Capacity
1957–69	28,500
1969–71	26,000
1971–76	24,000
1976–80	22,000
1980–84	19,175
1984–86	19,086
1986/87	12,130
1987/88	12,035
1988–90	12,708
1990–92	11,375
1992/93	11,428
1993–96	11,880
1996/97	11,000
1997/98	10,440
1998–2001	10,770
2001–03	12,000
2003–05	9,600
2005–08	9,776
2008–13	10,375
2013/14	9,287
2014/15	12,081
2015/16	11,464

Since 2005, a temporary stand has been erected (for certain games), increasing the capacity by more than 2,000. The capacity of Dorchester's ground, which the Cherries used in 2001, was 4,000.

PLASTIC PITCH FOOTY

Bournemouth have so far played five Football League games on artificial surfaces, drawing two, both at Preston, 0-0 in 1990/91 and 2-2 the following season, and losing three, all at Boundary Park against Oldham Athletic between 1987 and 1990, 2-0, 2-0 and 4-0. The Cherries scored just two goals while conceding ten.

NULL AND VOID

Bournemouth played three Third Division South games at the start of the ill-fated 1939/40 season. They beat Northampton Town 10-0, lost narrowly 2-1 at Notts County and were held to a 2-2 draw at Dean Court by Queens Park Rangers. These results were expunged from the record books due to the season being abandoned due to the World War Two.

PROFESSIONAL CLUB

Bournemouth FC became a professional club in 1910, the year they moved to Dean Court from their Castlemain Road ground in Pokesdown.

SIGN YOUR FULL NAME PLEASE!

In March 1993, Bournemouth had a player registered at the club who had 31 letters in his name – Peter Clifford William James Beadle. A Londoner born in May 1972, he was a forward with Gillingham and Tottenham Hotspur before scoring twice in nine league appearances for the Cherries. He left Dean Court for Southend United in March 1994, and later assisted Watford and Bristol Rovers. In September 1977, Cherries manager John Benson signed Ernest Forbes Phillipson-Masters on loan from Southampton. The Bournemouth-born defender, whose 29-letter name reads like a team's back four, scored twice in seven league appearances before returning to The Dell. He also played for Exeter City, Luton Town, Plymouth Argyle and Bristol City during his 12-year senior professional career from 1972–84. His best spell came with Plymouth for whom he had 119 league games in three seasons from 1979. Argentinian forward Francisco Enrique Gonsalez Peed (28 letters) was signed by Bournemouth in 1929 from Aston Villa. He played in two league games for the Cherries before transferring to Norwich City in 1930. He went on to play for Newport County, Shelbourne (Ireland), Barrow and Bath City. Another 28-letter Cherry was centre-forward Stewart Christopher Littlewood, born in Treeton in 1906, who scored 11 goals in 20 league games in the mid-1930s. Two other long-named stars are Chukwunyeaka Osundu Eribeen (25 letters), a Londoner, born in Westminster in 1980, who played 47 league games for the Cherries between 2000 and 2003, and another Londoner, Wayne Anthony Norman Talkes (24 letters), who joined the Cherries from Southampton in 1974. The midfielder from Ealing made 18 league appearances during his short career at the club. Also you can add James Theirs Harrison Lovie (24 letters), reserve team player William Thomas Arden McGann (24), Edmund William Alfred Smith (24), Derek Neville Lester Stroud (24), Wayne Anthony Norman Talkes (24), Miles Vivien Esifi Addison (23), Barrington Ronald Mansell (23), Derek Bryan Philip Rickard (23), Ferreira Rodrigues Daniel, known as Dani (23), Thomas Cansfield Southren (23), Michael Joseph McCulloch (22), George Ehialimolisa Ndah (22), Carroll Lloyd Richards (20), Franck Jacques Rolling (20), Efangwu Goziem Ekoku (18).

SHORTEST NAME

The player with the shortest name ever to play senior football for the Cherries is goalkeeper Lee Camp (seven letters). The following all have eight letters in their name: Leon Best, Jamie Day, Roy Gater, Ian Harte, Ian Leigh, Alex Moth and Marc Pugh. And two players with just three-letter surnames are Ian Cox and Ben Rix.

UNUSUAL NAMES

Apart from the many overseas-born players who have been signed by the Cherries, there are several non-foreigners (born in the UK) with quite unusual names who have also been associated with the club down the years. Here are a few, listed in A-Z order: Miles Vivien Esifi Addison, Artistide Basselle, Narada Bernard, Chukkie Eribenne, Iyseden Christie, David Houston Coleman, James De Garis, George Donowa (Southampton), Charlie Gallogly, Everald La Ronde (London), Dicky Milton Girling, Brandon Goodship, Milton Mackay Graham, Kezie Ibe, Sammy Igoe, Harry McGill Kinghorn, Kenny Listrem (Salford), James Theirs Harrison Lovie (Peterhead), Robert Nivison McGowan (Sanquhar/Dumfries), Jonathan Muleba, George Ehialimolisa Ndah (Dulwich), Marcus Oldbury (Bournemouth), Tom Gracie Paton (Saltcoats), Theophilus Enos 'Tot' Pike, Roy Proverbs, Lancelot Holliday Richardson, John Hardy Robson, Mark Schiavi, Dominic Shimmin, Leslie Taylor Sille (Liverpool), John Smeulders, Junior Stanislas, Jim Whelpton, David Woozley and Nico Yennaris.

B IS BEST FOR BRIAN

Midfielder Brian Smith, born in Bolton, played for five different teams during his career and all of them began with the letter B – his hometown club Bolton Wanderers (from 1971), Bradford City (1977), Blackpool (1979), Bournemouth (1980) and Bury (1982). He made a total of 122 league appearances, including 40 for the Cherries.

CHERRY PICKING HAMMERS

Over the course of time, several players, coaches and managers have been associated with both Bournemouth and West Ham United, and they include the following: John Arnott, Bobby Barnes, Mohamed Berthe, Ian Bishop, John Bond, Phil Brignull, George Collin, Jack Collison, Jermain Defoe, Anthony Edgar, Terrell Forbes, Dale Gordon, Trevor Hartley, Matt Holland, Bobby Howe, Stephen Jones, Bill Kitchener, Everard Le Ronde, Keith Miller, Paul Mitchell, Stuart Morgan, Jimmy

Neighbour, Manny Omoyinmi, Reg Parker, Gerry Peyton, Gary Pugh, Stephen Purches, Jimmy Quinn, Harry Redknapp, Keith Rowland, Gary Russo, Mark Schiavi, Tony Scott, Tommy Southren, Jamie Victory, Mark Watson, David Webb (Hammers amateur), Jim Whelpton (Hammers trialist) and Jimmy Wood (Cherries reserve).

WE WILL RETURN

Among the players who, over the last 80 years or so, have had two separate spells with Bournemouth, we have: David Best (1960–66: 1975, 232 league appearances): Micky Cave (1971/72: 1977, 141 appearances): Richard Cooke (1987–89: 1991/92, 125 appearances): Steve Fletcher (1992–2007: 2009–13, 628 appearances): Howard Goddard (1974–76: 1981/82: 73 appearances): Max-Alain Gradel (2007-08: 2015-16): Tom Heffernan (1979–83: 1985-87, 217 appearances): Steve Jones (1994–96: 1997/98, 79 appearances): Josh McQuoid (2006–11: 2012–15), Paul Mitchell (1989–93: 1996, 16 appearances): Trevor Morgan (1980/81: 1982–84, 141 appearances): Mark Nightingale (1974–76: 1982–86, 199 appearances): Martin O'Connor (1985–90: 1993–95, 186 appearances): David Puckett (1986–88: 1992, 39 appearances): Tony Pulis (1986–89: 1990/91): Harry Redknapp (1972–76: 1982 – then manager): Fawzi Saadi (2002–04: 2005/06), Mark Schiavi (1983: 1984/85: 29 apps), James White (1957–59: 1966–70, 177 appearances) and Paul Wood (1991: 1991–94, 99 appearances). Two goalkeepers – Neil Moss and John Smeulders – both had three spells with the club. Moss played in 1993–95, 2002 and 2003–08, making 185 league appearances, and Smeulders in 1979/80, 1984–86 and 1987/88, lining up in 98 league games.

CLOSE TO A BAKER'S DOZEN

Rampant Bournemouth crushed managerless Birmingham City 8-0 at St Andrews and then doubled up by winning 4-2 at the Goldsands Stadium in the two Championship games between the clubs in the 2014/15 season. A crowd of 13,837 saw Brett Pitman put the Cherries ahead inside three minutes in Birmingham before the Blues had defender David Edgar red-carded for a foul on Callum Wilson. After that it was one-way traffic. Wilson and Matt Ritchie made it 3-0 by half-time before the Cherries ran riot in the second period. Marc Pugh netted a hat-trick and two more from substitute Tokelo Rantie, the first a penalty, completed Birmingham's misery. In addition, Paul Caddis had a spot-kick saved by Bournemouth goalkeeper Artur Boruc with the score at 3-0. For the Blues it was their heaviest home defeat – in April 1960 they crashed 7-1 to neighbours West Bromwich Albion – and it was also their heaviest league defeat at home or away, in terms of goal difference, since losing

9-1 at Sheffield Wednesday in December 1930. When the teams met in the return fixture at the Goldsands Stadium, the Blues shot into a 2-0 lead inside 21 minutes before Steve Cook (39) and Wilson (45) drew the Cherries level before half-time. A penalty converted by Yann Kermorgant soon after the restart put Bournemouth in front before Charlie Daniels sealed victory with a fourth goal 15 minutes from time. The Blues once again finished with ten men, skipper Paul Robinson taking an early bath late on. A crowd of 11,084 saw Eddie Howe's men shoot to the top of the table after this second win.

PAUL MORRELL –
PLAYER TO PROBATION OFFICER

Paul Morrell, born in Poole in March 1961, played for local side Dexter Sports before signing for his hometown club in August 1977. In February 1980 he joined Bath City for £3,000 and, after representing the Southern League, switched his allegiance to nearby Weymouth in August 1981. Two years later, Paul signed for Bournemouth and over the next decade made 343 league appearances for the Cherries, scoring the winning goal in the 1984 Associate Members Cup Final against Hull City. After a spell in Hong Kong, he returned to the UK to manage his former club Poole Town up to May 2004. Paul is now a probation officer, based in Bournemouth. His brother, Peter, also played for Poole Town, as well as Hamworthy United, Weymouth and Dorchester Town.

DOWSETT – TOP MAN

One of the finest goalscorers of his era, Dicky Dowsett was born in Chelmsford, Essex, in July 1931. He began his career at non-league club Sudbury Town as a winger before joining Tottenham Hotspur in May 1952. He scored in his only league outing for the London club, against Aston Villa in August 1954. Transferred to Southend United in May 1955, he went on to net four times in 20 matches for the Shrimpers in 1955/56 and, while at Roots Hall, he was spotted by Frank Dudley, who recommended him to his former colleague Ted Bates, who was then manager at Southampton. Dowsett joined Saints in July 1956, and featured in two League matches and one FA Cup tie but was unable to stake a claim for a regular place in the first team. Sold to Bournemouth for just £100 in June 1957, Dowsett was converted into an inside-forward with great success by his boss Freddie Cox, and over the next five years, became a star performer, top-scoring on three occasions. Described as being 'determined, fast and useful in the air', he found the net on 79 occasions in 169 matches for the Cherries, and was featured on the club's logo. In November 1962, he joined Crystal Palace for a fee of £3,500 and at Selhurst Park notched up a further 22 goals in 54 outings. In June 1965, Dowsett entered non-league football with Weymouth and, after helping the Dorset club win the Southern League championship for the second successive season, he retired in 1968, at the age of 37. Within a month or so, Dowsett had returned to Dean Court as the club's commercial manager, holding the post from June 1968 until March 1985 (when Brian Tiler took over), and during the mid-1980s his wife served as Bournemouth's club secretary. A member of the Dorset Cricket Society, Dowsett became a part-time after-dinner speaker, recalling his experiences during his career as a professional footballer which realised almost 130 goals in 265 competitive games, 106 coming in 246 league appearances.

RELIABILITY TO THE FULL

John Bond in 1971/72, John Benson in 1976/77 and Brian Tiler in 1986/87 each used only 20 players in Football League games in the seasons given. Twenty-two were utilised in 1970/71, 1975/76, 1977/78, 1978/79, 1984/85 and 2003/04, while 23 took the field during 1979/80, 1981/82 and 1997/98. And going right back to the start of Bournemouth's ventures in league football, 22 were called up in 1923/24.

BRISTOL FASHION

Bournemouth scored no fewer than 17 goals in the four league games played against the two Bristol clubs in 1985/86. They battered City 5-0 at home (with a Colin Clarke hat-trick) and defeated them 3-1 at Ashton Gate, and whipped Rovers 6-1 at Dean Court and edged out a 3-2 victory at the Eastville Stadium. Clarke netted five of the goals and Russell four.

GOAL SHY

Twenty of Bournemouth's 46 league games in the 1992/93 season were goalless at half-time. In the end, when the final ball was kicked, the Cherries had failed to score in 16 of their matches; their opponents in 12, while six of the fixtures finished level at 0-0, four at Dean Court. Both encounters against Wigan Athletic failed to produce a single goal. The Cherries, in fact, managed less than a goal a game and came 17th in the division.

TEAM COLOURS

The design and colours of Bournemouth's current striped shirts, red and black, first introduced in 1971, are based on the old AC Milan strip. Over the last 40 years or so, certainly since major kit sponsorship, advertising and TV coverage has increased, Bournemouth have had their fair share of change strips, and here are a few of the many colourful strips (mainly shirts) the players have donned away from home: blue and yellow halves; white tops; all yellow; white tops with red strip down side; white with red trim; green and black stripes; navy and sky blue stripes; blue and black stripes; all black with yellow trim, royal blue tops with black shorts and purple shirts with green and navy blue trimmings. And at odd times there have been a few more colourful jerseys.

RED-HOT PITMAN

Brett Pitman scored in eight consecutive league games for the Cherries between 12 March and 20 April 2012. He netted, in turn, against Stevenage (away), Oldham Athletic (away), Bury (home), Colchester United (away), Scunthorpe United (home), Notts County (home), Shrewsbury Town (away) and Carlisle United (home). His strikes at Stevenage, Oldham and Colchester, and at home to Scunthorpe, earned 1-0 victories and the Cherries were unbeaten in all eight games. In August 2010, Pitman netted a hat-trick in a quarter of an hour (50–65 minutes) in Bournemouth's 5-1 home league win over Peterborough United.

ONE MATCH WONDERS!

Since entering the Football League in 1923, scores of players have made just one senior appearance for Bournemouth (some as a substitute). Among them we have: David Adekola, Rupert Blezzard, Billy Bow, Billy Cameron, George Donowa, Chris Ferrett, Matt Finlay, Amos Foyewa, Billy Francis, Hayward, Danny Holmes (as a substitute), Steve Hutchings (sub), Jamie Jenkins (sub), David Kevan (sub), Tom Liddle, Bob McAlinden, Bob McDonald, Norman McKay, Sid Miles, David Morris (sub), Ryan Moss (sub), Rob Newman (sub), Roy O'Brien, Conal Platt, John Rose, Gary Russo, Michael Standing, Marek Stech, Anthony Stephens, George Stevens, Gareth Stewart, Jack Sutton, Harold Tarrant, Bill Tyler, Harry Walker, Trevor Wallbridge (sub), George Webb, David Wells (sub), Jim Whelpton, Jamie Whisken, Ken Whiteside, Charlie Wilkinson, David Williams, Gareth Williams (sub) and Bob Young. Neil Prosser made two appearances, one as a substitute.

ROBINS LOVE CHERRIES!

Bournemouth led Swindon Town 2-0 in a Third Division South game on 2 January 1926, but it all went wrong for the Cherries after the interval as the rampant Robins stormed back to win 8-2, Frank Richardson scoring a four-timer for the winners.

THIRD DIVISION SOUTH CUP RECORD

Bournemouth competed in the annual 1930s Third Division South Cup competition on six occasions, the details being:

1933/34	Bristol City, home (won 7-1)	2,766
	Northampton Town, home (lost 2-1)	2,912
1934/35	Swindon Town, home (won 3-0)	2,129
	Coventry City, home (lost 5-2)	1,059
1935/36	Clapton Orient, away (drew 1-1)	3,335
	Clapton Orient, home (won 6-2)	2,089
	Bristol City, home (won 1-0)	2,261
	Coventry City, away (lost 3-2)	2,101
1936/37	Luton Town, away (lost 3-1)	4,076
1937/38	Reading, home (lost 2-1)	2,125
1938/39	Exeter City, away (won 2-1)	1,007
	Queens Park Rangers, away (lost 3-2)	2,034
1945/46	Queens Park Rangers, home (drew 1-1)	12,786
	Queens Park Rangers, away (won 1-0)	14,992
	Walsall, neutral (won 1-0 in final)	19,715

CHERRY REDS

The following have all been associated with both Bournemouth and Manchester United as players, managers and coaches: Russell Beardsmore, George Best, Chris Casper, Frank Fidler, Don Givens, Bob Green, Ray Hampson, Josh King, John O'Shea, Ted MacDougall, Mark Rawlinson, Lance Richardson, Jack Rowley, Mel Simmonds, Paul Theather and Graeme Tomlinson.

FAMILY AFFAIR

Jack Rowley (born in Wolverhampton in 1918, died 1998) was a centre-forward who played for Wolves and Cradley Heath prior to joining Bournemouth in February 1937. He scored 12 goals in 22 league appearances for the Cherries before transferring to Manchester United in October 1937. He went on to net 208 goals in 458 first-class games for United (182 in 380 league appearances) up to February 1955 when he moved to Plymouth. Only three players have claimed more goals for the Reds than Rowley, who won the league championship and FA Cup with United, gained six full England caps, two more in wartime football, played for his country's B team and represented the Football League. After retiring in 1956, Rowley managed Argyle, Oldham Athletic (two spells), AFC Ajax, Wrexham and Bradford Park Avenue, being in charge for a total of 504 games. Jack's brother Arthur Rowley (also born in Wolverhampton in 1925, died in 2002) holds the record for scoring more league goals than any other player – 434 in 619 games between 1946 and 1965, playing for West Bromwich Albion, Fulham, Leicester and Shrewsbury, the latter as player-manager. Between them the Rowley brothers scored no less than 717 goals in 1,202 club matches. The Redknapps – Harry (father) and Jamie (son) – appeared in a combined total of 567 league games (46 goals) during their professional careers. Harry made 102 appearances for the Cherries, while Jamie made just 13. Jamie's brother, Mark, played non-league football for Bashley, but a knee injury ended his career somewhat prematurely. John Bond (father) and his son (Kevin) amassed a grand total of 1,048 league appearances during their combined careers. Bond senior made 511 and Kevin accumulated 537, which included 126 for Bournemouth. Twins George Fisher (Millwall, Fulham and Colchester United) and John Fisher (Millwall and Bournemouth) both played professionally between 1946 and 1960. John made 52 league appearances for the Cherries from 1949–52. Between them the Fisher twins played in a grand total of 471 league games. David Regis, who made six appearances on loan for Bournemouth from Plymouth Argyle in 1992, is the brother of the former West Bromwich Albion, Aston Villa, Wolves and England striker Cyrille Regis MBE, the uncle of Jason Roberts, also ex-West Brom, Blackburn Rovers and Reading, and cousin of British athlete John Regis MBE. The brothers Haines from Ynysybwl in Wales – Mervyn, born in May 1923 and Don, born in September 1925, were players together at Bournemouth in 1948/49. They were released at the end of the campaign without breaking into the first team. Later they ended up together at Newport County (1950/51). Full-back Phil Ferns, born in Liverpool in November 1937, played for the Merseyside club, Bournemouth (1965/66) and Mansfield Town. He was followed into Dean Court 13 years later by his son, also named Phil. He, too, was born in Liverpool in September 1961, and made over 100 appearances for the Cherries (95 in the league) as a left-back before moving to Charlton Athletic in 1981, later assisting Wimbledon, Blackpool and Aldershot. The Ferns accumulated 340 league appearances between them (11 goals). Two of the three Mundee brothers played for Bournemouth – Brian in 1982 and Denny in 1988–92 (100 league appearances). The third brother, Barry, played at a semi-professional level. Brothers James and Kevin White, both of whom were born in Poole in 1942 and 1948 respectively, were players together at Bournemouth from 1966–68. Bill Colley's father was a reserve team player with Wolves (1906–07); John Bradford's cousin, Bill, played for Birmingham and Walsall in the 1920s and Billy Rafferty's brother, Stewart, starred for several Scottish clubs during the 1960s and 70s. South African-born striker Mark Stein, who played for Bournemouth on loan in March, April and May 1998, scoring four goals in 11 league appearances, was the brother of Brian and Eddie (Ed). Mark, an England youth international,

HARRY REDKNAPP

and Brian, who gained one full cap for England, won the League Cup with Luton Town against Arsenal in 1988. Between them the three Stein brothers made a total of 812 league appearances and netted 261 goals. Luke Summerfield, a Bournemouth player in 2006/07, is the son of the former West Bromwich Albion, Walsall, Cardiff City, Exeter City, Birmingham City, Shrewsbury Town and Plymouth Argyle striker Kevin Summerfield. Blair Sturrock, who was a Cherry in 2009/10, is the son of the former Scottish international Paul Sturrock, ex-Dundee United, who won 20 full caps for his country. Charlie Sheringham, who scored once in six league games for Bournemouth (2011–13), is the son of the former Millwall, Nottingham Forest, Manchester United, Tottenham Hotspur, West Ham and England striker Teddy Sheringham. Bournemouth's 1981 loanee Dave Madden and Lawrie Madden, who served with several clubs, including Leicester City, Sheffield Wednesday and Wolves, were both born in London, and were related. Shaun Brooks, who starred for Bournemouth between 1987 and 1994, making almost 150 appearances, is the son of former Spurs, Chelsea and England international forward of the 1950s, Johnny Brooks. Ex-player Dicky Dowsett and his wife worked together behind the scenes at Dean Court in the mid-1980s.

PLAYERS GALORE

Since the Cherries joined the Football League for the 1923/24 season, just over 600 players (some on loan) have been associated with the club and most have appeared in the first team at competitive level. The surname of over 70 of these players starts with the letter B; more than 60 with the letter S, more than 50 with the letters C and M, and over 40 with G. The only Cherries players whose surnames begin with the letters Q and Z are Jimmy Quinn and Stephane Zubar, while there have been two beginning with Y and four with V.

NO, NOT 007!

Timothy Dalton was a goalkeeper (not a secret agent actor) born in London in 1965, who played for the Cherries in the 1980s as well as for Coventry City, Notts County, Bradford City, Tranmere Rovers, Gillingham, Boston United and a handful of clubs in Ireland, winning medals with both Derry City and Portadown.

IT'S 'B' FOR BOURNEMOUTH

It's always nice to think (even assume) what might have been. If I could choose my own team perhaps, sign the players who would like in my squad, these would be my two 'B' surname line-ups for the Cherries –

covering the period from 1970 through to 2015 – to play against each other (fictitiously of course) and I'm sure both would do a good job in League football as well. Team 'A' – Boruc; Broadhurst, R. Brown, K. Bond, Browning, Beardsmore, Bishop, Bradbury, Blissett, Boyer and G. Best, plus five substitutes, namely K. Baker, Barnes, Borthwick, Bryant and K. Brown with John Bond as manager. Team 'B'- Bartram; G. Butler, Brignull, Bailey, Benson (player-manager), Beck, Miller, Brissett, Brookes, Barton and M. Butler, along with five substitutes, Begovic, Buttle, Bridge, Bartley and Button. The result would be a 0-0 draw with defences dominating throughout the 90 minutes!

M SQUAD

And how about this Bournemouth team of Ms covering the last 45 years: Moss; Masters, Morrell, Maher, Morris, Machin, Mitchell, McQuoid, MacDonald, MacDougall, Moulden. Subs: Marshall (gk), Massey, Mundee, McGorry, Morgan. Manager: McGarry.

POOLE TOWN LINK

There have been quite a few players who have served both Bournemouth and Poole Town. Here are several who have been associated with the Dolphins, and there are many Cherries among them: Jimmy Allen*, Charlie Austin, Alan Banks, Sammy Beswick, Ken Boyes, Charlie Brown, Roger Brown, Marcus Browning*, Alec Campbell, Graham Carr, Brian Chambers (player-manager), Jack Coxford, Billy Coxon, Max Cream, Warren Cummings*, Horace Cumner*, Jimmy Daws, Stuart Douglas, John Evanson, Tony Funnell, Peter Gordon, Jackie Henderson*, Ken Hodgson, Joe Hutton, Andy Jones*, Tony Knapp, Ted MacDougall*, Wilf Mannion*, Jimmy McDonald, Thomas McGhee, Bobby Mason, Ralph Miller, Doug Millward, Paul Morrell (also Dolphins manager), Brian Mundee, Jimmy Munro, Brian O'Donnell, Harry Osman, Pat Parker, Carl Pettefer, Len Phillips*, Tony Priscott, Ernie Pym, Fred Rhodes, Stan Rickaby*, Jim Rollo, Barry Rowan, Fawzi Saadi, John Smeulders and Peter Wakeman. Jimmy Glass became Poole's goalkeeping coach.
* These players won full international caps.

GAMES AGAINST POOLE

Bournemouth and Poole Town have met four times in the FA Cup. In the first game, played in 1909/10, the Cherries lost 3-2 in a qualifying encounter. They then recorded two victories, 2-0 in a replay in 1910/11 (after a 1-1 draw) and 4-1 in the first round in 1928/29, when just over 1,000 spectators attended Poole's local community ground in late

November. Prior to the start of the never-to-be-forgotten 2014/15 season, the Cherries' youth team lost 2-0 to Poole in a testimonial.

ABANDONED MATCHES

With 5,000 fans inside Fellows Park, and Bournemouth 1-0 up on Walsall in a Third Division South encounter in November 1952, the referee abandoned the game in the 42nd minute due to the inclement weather. The re-arranged match – played in April 1953 in front of 3,857 spectators – resulted in a 2-2 draw. The Saddlers finished bottom of the table and had to apply (successfully) for re-election. After a battling 0-0 draw with Newcastle United at Dean Court in an FA Cup third round tie in January 1992, Bournemouth were frustrated when the replay at St James' Park was abandoned through fog after just 17 minutes play with a blank scoresheet (See under: More FA Cup Facts).

FIRST BLACK PLAYER

One of the first black players – if not the first – to appear in a Football League game for Bournemouth was John 'Eddie' Parris, a Welsh international outside-left, born in Pwllmeyric in January 1911, who scored 23 goals in 100 league appearances for the Cherries in the mid-1930s. He also played for Bradford Park Avenue, Luton Town, Northampton Town and Cheltenham Town, and won one cap for his country. He died in 1971, aged 59.

LONG DISTANCE TRAVELLERS

Eddie Prudham was born in Felling, Tyne and Wear, in April 1952 and started his career as a junior with Sheffield Wednesday, 107 miles from his home town. In 1974, aged 22, he left Hillsborough and returned north to Carlisle United (156 miles away), and after loan spells with two other northern clubs, Hartlepool United (1976) and Workington (1977), he moved from Brunton Park to Stockport County (128 miles) and then, in May 1980, he ventured another 251 miles south to Bournemouth. A forward, he played in just four league games before leaving Dean Court in the summer of 1981 to become a probation officer, later entering the prison service. During his near-20-year career from 1966, striker Billy Rafferty played for two clubs in the north-east (Carlisle United and Newcastle United), three in the south (Bournemouth, Plymouth Argyle and Portsmouth), two in the Midlands (Coventry City and Wolves), plus Blackpool and Port Glasgow. And Ken Oliver, an inside-forward born in Scotland in 1938, played for Sunderland and South Shields in the north, Barnsley in Yorkshire, Watford in Hertfordshire, then Workington in Cumbria before having a spell with Bournemouth in 1967.

HOPE FOR O'NEILL

Inside-forward Alan Hope, born near Sunderland in November 1937, started his career with his hometown club. At the age of 19, Hope changed his surname to O'Neill (after his mother had re-married) and he spent the rest of his playing days under that name. He left Sunderland for Aston Villa in 1960, switched to Plymouth Argyle in 1962 and played for Bournemouth from February 1964 to May 1965 (netting eight goals in 37 starts). He ended up with Cambridge United and now lives in the Bournemouth area.

HEAVIEST DEFEATS

Bournemouth suffered their heaviest defeat at competitive level in December 1982 when they were battered 9-0 by Lincoln City in a Third Division game in front of 3,597 spectators at Sincil Bank. Derek Bell and Gordon Hobson (later to play for Southampton) both scored hat-tricks for the Imps, who fired in seven goals in the second half as the Cherries were gobbled up. And it didn't end there as Bournemouth crashed 5-0 at Leyton Orient in the next away game. Bournemouth's previous heaviest league defeat was at Valley Parade in January 1970 when they crashed 8-1 against Bradford City. The Bantams led 6-0 at half-time as Bobby Ham scored a hat-trick in this one-sided encounter.

BIGGEST WINS

Bournemouth's biggest win in competitive football is 11-0 against Margate in the first round of the FA Cup at Dean Court in November 1971. A crowd of 12,079 at Dean Court saw Ted MacDougall score a record nine goals against the non-league club that afternoon including one from the penalty spot. The other scorers were Mel Machin and Micky Cave. The Cherries' line-up that day was: Davies; Machin, Kitchener, Benson, Jones, Powell, Cave, Boyer, MacDougall, Miller, Scott (sub: De Garis). The team ousted Southend United 2-0 in the next round, but fell at the next hurdle, beaten 1-0 at Walsall. 'SuperMac' scored another six FA Cup goals in Bournemouth's 8-1 win over Oxford City in a first round replay in November 1970. In September 1956, Bournemouth defeated Swindon Town 7-0 in a home Third Division South game and they eclipsed this winning margin of victory with an emphatic 8-0 win over Birmingham City at St Andrews in a Championship game in October 2014. The Cherries beat Northampton Town 10-0 in a home Third Division South game in September 1939, but this result was expunged from the record books after the competition was abandoned due to the outbreak of the World War Two. A Dean Court crowd of 3,000 saw Patsy Gallacher (2),

Jack Kirkham (3), Bob Redfern (2), Fred Marsden, Bill Tunnicliffe and Tom Paton score for the Cherries, who led 3-0 at half-time. During the previous week this same Northampton team had defeated Swindon 1-0 and lost 2-1 at home to Exeter City, while the Cherries had lost 2-1 at Notts County and drew 2-2 with Queens Park Rangers.

LONG JOURNEYS

The longest journey any Bournemouth team has made to play a Football League match, or indeed, compete in a cup tie, is 361 miles, north to Newcastle United's St James' Park ground, a good six-hour trip by road. The Cherries lost on their first visit to Newcastle, going down 3-0 in a Second Division game in February 1990. The distance to Carlisle United's Brunton Park ground is 359 miles; to Sunderland's Roker Park or Stadium of Light (since 1997) it is 352.4 miles; to Hartlepool United's Victoria Park it is 337.5 miles and the distance to Middlesbrough's Riverside (or Ayresome Park prior to 1995) is 267 miles.

CARRYING THE BOURNEMOUTH FLAG

Bournemouth's former Blackpool and England B centre-half Johnny Crosland starred for the Third Division South side against the Third Division North in the annual fixture in March 1955 and was on the winning side, 2-0 at Elm Park, Reading, before 7,050 fans. In October 1956, in this same fixture, Cherries forward Stan Newsham helped the South team win 2-1 in front of 14,500 spectators at Highfield Road, Coventry. And in April 1957, Cherries left-winger Reg Cutler played for the South XI in a 2-1 defeat in front of 12,362 spectators at Edgeley Park, Stockport.

TWO GOLDEN OLDIES

In season 1928/29, former Bournemouth manager Harry Kinghorn, who at the time was 42 years of age and the official trainer at Dean Court, was asked to come out of retirement and play on the left wing. Ex-Bristol Rovers and Leicester goalkeeper Joe Calvert was 41 when he made his 119th and final league appearance of his career for Watford against Bournemouth in 1948. Possibly the oldest opponent ever to face the Cherries at senior level, he didn't have a great day, ending up on the losing side 3-0.

BIG AWAY WIN... AND A DOUBLE

Bournemouth were outstanding at times during the 1972/73 season and their best away win came at Rotherham in October when they whipped the Millers 7-2 with goals from Brian Clark (4), Alan Groves (2) and Micky

Cave. The Cherries moved into second place in the Third Division table. Later in the season the Cherries completed the double over Rotherham by winning 4-0 at Dean Court, with Cave again on target.

FESTIVAL OF BRITAIN MATCHES

In 1951, to celebrate the Festival of Britain, like most other clubs north and south of the border, Bournemouth played two friendly matches against foreign opposition. In mid-May they drew 2-2 at home with the French side AS Nancy and four days later lost 1-0 to the German outfit Hamborn 07, also at Dean Court.

POOR RUN

Bournemouth were knocked out of the FA Cup in the first round four seasons running between 1974 and 1978, losing, in turn, to Wycombe Wanderers, Sutton Town, Newport County and Colchester United. They fell at the second hurdle in 1978/79 and 1979/80 to Wimbledon and Colchester, again, respectively.

POINTING THE WAY

The highest number of points gained by the Cherries in a League season is 97 – in the Third Division in 1986/87. The Cherries banked 90 in 2014/15, 88 in 1981/82, 83 in 2010/11 and again in 2012/13, and 76 in 1998/99. The most points the team collected under the two points for a win rule was 62, in the Third Division in 1971/72. And the lowest points tally to date has been just 27 in 1933/34.

GOALS GALORE

Bournemouth set a new club record in 2014/15 by scoring 142 goals in 60 first team games. The Cherries notched 98 in the Championship, six in the FA Cup, 11 in the League Cup and 27 in friendlies. In fact, this was the first time Bournemouth had netted more than a century of goals in competitive matches for 58 years, and it was on-loan striker Kenwyne Jones who had the pleasure of heading the 100th of the campaign – the crucial equaliser in the 1-1 Good Friday league draw at Ipswich. Also, a total of 143 goals was scored in Bournemouth's 46 home and away league games in 2014/15 – 73 at the Goldsands Stadium, 48 by the Cherries. The biggest league victories in 2014/15 were those of 8-0 at Birmingham, 6-1 at Blackpool, 5-1 at Fulham and 4-0 at Huddersfield, plus 5-3 v. Cardiff City and 4-0 v. Blackpool at home. Back in 1956/57, the Cherries netted 88 league goals in the Third Division South, 19 in the FA Cup and five in friendlies for a total of 112. Their biggest league wins were 7-0 v. Swindon Town, 6-1 v. Millwall, 6-1 v. Shrewsbury Town at home, and 4-0 v. Reading and 4-3 v. Millwall away. The 46 League games played that season realised, 150 goals, 77 of which were scored at Dean Court, 57 of them by the Cherries. The most league goals conceded by Bournemouth in a season is 102 (37 at home, 65 away) in 1933/34.

ENGLAND INTERNATIONALS

The following players, who all gained full England international caps, were associated with Bournemouth during their respective careers: Darren Anderton (30 caps), David Armstrong (three), James Beattie (trialist, five), Ryan Bertrand (three*), Herbert Bliss (one), Luther Blissett (14), Phil Boyer (one), Jermain Defoe (55), Rio Ferdinand (81), Charlie George (one), Gordon Hill (trialist/trainee, six), Adam Lallana (12*), Bill McGarry (four), Vincent Matthews (two), Chris Powell (trial, five), Jamie Redknapp (17), Kevin Reeves (two), Graham Roberts (six), Jack Rowley (guest, six), John Smith (three) and Don Welsh (three). Sam Beswick and World War Two guest Lester Finch both won England amateur caps. Other Bournemouth managers (apart from Bill McGarry) who played in full internationals for England were John Bruton (three caps) and Bob Crompton (41) while Reg Flewin and Don Welsh represented their country during World War Two. Two more ex-England stars – Ken Brown (one cap) and Arthur Cunliffe (two) – were both engaged as trainers at Dean Court. * Still adding to their total as at 2015.

ON THE INTERNATIONAL FRONT

Of the many other players who have been associated with Bournemouth and also represented their country at senior level, we have the following:
Bosnia & Herzegovina: Asmir Begovic (40 caps*)
Brittany/France: Yann Kermorgant (one)
Ghana: Christian Atsu (five*)
Guadeloupe: Stephane Zubar (two)
Ivory Coast: Max-Alain Gradel (41*)
Liberia: Chris Wreh (36)
Lichtenstein: Benjamin Bucher (five)
Nigeria: Efan Ekoku (20)
Northern Ireland: George Best (37), Lee Camp (ten*), Tommy Casey (12), Colin Clarke (30), Warren Feeney (46), Charlie Gallogly (two), Billy Hughes (one), Dick Keith (23), Joe Miller (three), Dudley Milligan (one), Jimmy Quinn (46), Steve Robinson (seven) and Keith Rowland (19)
Norway: Jo Tessem (nine)
Poland: Artur Boruc (59*)

MATT RITCHIE

Republic of Ireland: Harry Arter (two*), Leon Best (seven), Nick Colgan (nine), David Forde (19*), Don Givens (56), Tommy Godwin (13), Ian Harte (64), Gary Howlett (one), David Langan (26), Terry Murray (one), Roy O'Brien (five), Sean O'Driscoll (three), John O'Shea (100*), Alex Pearce (one*) and Gerry Peyton (33)

Scotland: James A. Blair (one), Jimmy Blair (eight), Warren Cummings (one), Jimmy Gabriel (two), Peter Grant (two), Richard Hughes (five), Ted MacDougall (seven), John McKenzie (nine), Matt Ritchie (four*) and Paul Telfer (one)

South Africa: Tokelo Rantie (26)

Trinidad & Tobago: Kenwyne Jones (68*)

USA: Frank Simek (five)

Wales: Marcus Browning (five), Jack Collison (16), Carl Fletcher (16), Andy Jones (six), David Jones (eight), Shaun MacDonald (one), Eddie Parris (one), Eddie Perry (three), Derek Showers (two), Neil Slatter (22), Brian Stock (three), Sam Vokes (33*) and David Williams (five)

Yugoslavia: Ivan Golac (1)

• Still adding to total as at September 2015.

POINTS OF NATIONAL INTEREST

Billy Elliott (Bournemouth, 1937/38) played in one World War Two and one Victory International for England. He also represented the Army, FA and Western Command. Steve Robinson, born in Lisburn, also represented his country at schoolboy, Under-16, Under-18, Under-21, B and senior levels. He was a Cherry from 1994–98 during which time he scored 52 goals in 241 league appearances. Goalkeeper Gerry Peyton holds the record for being Bournemouth's most-capped player, making seven appearances for the Republic of Ireland as a Cherry (1986–91). Birmingham-born, he appeared in 202 league games for the club. Kenwyne Jones had scored 18 goals for Trinidad & Tobago up to May 2015.

HONOURED CHERRIES

Players not listed on 'The International Front' who have been associated with Bournemouth, and who gained amateur and/or semi-professional caps during their careers respective include:

England: Stephen Butten, Kevin Charlton, Peter Feeley, Trevor Finnigan, Scott Guyett, Shwan Jalal, Neil Merrick, Mark Newson, Carroll Richards, Peter Shearer, Shaun Teale, Peter Thompson and Matt Tubbs

Wales: Tony Nelson

And among the many post-World War Two players who had links with the Cherries at sometime or another during their respective careers, and gained schoolboy, youth, Under-19, Under-21, Under-23 and/or B caps for their country without gaining full honours include:

Australia: Scott McDonald

England: Miles Addison, Ryan Allsop, Ian Andrews, Warren Aspinall, Bobby Barnes, Frank Barton, Russell Beardsmore, David Bennett, Kenny Bird, Ian Bishop, Lee Bradbury, Phil Brignull, Shaun Brooks, Lee Camp, Jimmy Case, Chris Casper, Brian Chambers, Richard Cooke, Stephen Cooke, Johnny Crosland, Jamie Cureton, Jamie Day, Martin Duffield, Wayne Fereday, John Flood, Simon Francis, Ryan Garry, Neil Hague, Phil Holder, Eddie Howe, John Impey, Danny Ings, Shwan Jahal, Roger Jones, Phil Kite, Scott Malone, Martin McGrath, Andy Marshall, Les Melville, Paul Mitchell, Paul Moulden, George Ndah, Mark Nightingale, Manny Omoyinmi, Gavin Peacock, Roger Peters, Adrian Randall, Liam Ridgewell, Kevin Russell, John Sainty, Tony Scott, Adam Smith, Brian Smith, David Smith, John Smeulders, Michael Standing, Brian Statham, Mark Stein, Gareth Stewart, Andrew Surman, Paul Teather, Ron Tilsed, Neil Townsend, Reg Trim, Alex Watson, James White and Alan Whittle

Italy: Filippo Costa

Northern Ireland: Neil Masters

Republic of Ireland: Owen Coll, Steven Foley-Sheridan, Tom Keane, Michael McElhatton, Donal McDermott, Martin O'Connor, Eunan O'Kane and Tony Scully

Portugal: Diogo Andrade

Scotland: Josh Carmichael, Ryan Fraser and Robert Murray

Wales: Fred Davies, Jonathan Meads, Jonathan Moore, Joe Partington, Brian Stock and Rhoys Wiggins

Southern League XI: Paul Morrell

And, for the record, two Bournemouth players – Simon Francis and Matt Ritchie – were named in the Championship Team of the season for 2014/15, while Danny Ings played for England in the European U21 Championships in the Czech Republic.

DOUBLE WINNERS

Two stars who helped Arsenal complete the league and FA Cup double in 1970/71 – Charlie George and Eddie Kelly – both later played for Bournemouth. George was at the club in March 1982 and played in two games, while Kelly was a Cherry from August–December 1981 and was given 13 outings.

KEEPING UP WITH THE JONESES

Nine men named Jones have played first team football for the Cherries: Andy (40 appearances in 1990/91), Brynley (118 appearances, 1960–63), David (134 appearances, 1970–74), Jack (11 appearances in 1938/39),

Mickey Jones (six appearances in 1927/28), Kenwyne (six appearances on loan in 2014/15), Norman (three appearances as a guest goalkeeper in 1945/46); Roger (160 appearances, also in goal, 1965–70) and Steve (79 appearances, in two spells, 1994–96; 1997/98). Loanee Chris Jones was registered with the club in 2005, but didn't play. The club has been served by seven Smiths as well.

CELEBRITY FANS

Perhaps two of the better-known celebrity fans of the Cherries are Matt Tong, the drummer of the British indie rock band Bloc Party, and the Canadian-born film star, writer and comedian Seth Rogen who actually pulled the club's name out of a hat on Soccer AM to become a supporter!

SALARIES

The annual salary for a Bournemouth first team squad member in 2014/15 ranged from £340,000 to £425,000 with an average around £380,000. A few years earlier it was between £295,000 and £397,500. If one would like to know, in more detail, what a player is paid, these figures might knock you back a bit. A player earning £375,000 a year will receive approximately £31,250 a month; £7,211 a week; roughly £1,300 a day; £55 an hour; 92p a minute or 14p a second. And when he plays for 90 minutes in a match (taking out the half-time break) he stands to collect £89. At 2015, Barcelona superstar Lionel Messi was earning £29.1m a year; Cristiano Ronaldo £26.8m, Wayne Rooney £15.4m and Zlatan Ibrahimovic £14m. These figures are common knowledge on the internet, but there are, of course, other players around the world who could well be earning similar amounts of money.

GETTING INTO THE 'MOULD'

As a youngster, striker Paul Moulden got into the Guinness Book of Records after scoring no less than 340 goals (289 in the local league) for Bolton Boys' Club in 1981/82. He joined Manchester City in 1984 and, after gaining 15 England youth caps, moved to Bournemouth for £160,000 in 1989. After netting 13 goals in 32 league games for the Cherries, he switched his allegiance to Oldham Athletic a year later, played on loan with Brighton & Hove Albion in 1992, and rounded off his career with spells at Birmingham City (1993-95), Huddersfield Town (1995/96), Rochdale, Accrington Stanley and Bacup Borough, retiring in 2000.

AMATEUR ROAMER

Liverpool-born outside-left Leslie Sille was an amateur footballer who made just five league appearances while serving with four different clubs in two seasons (1946–48): Tranmere Rovers, Bournemouth (one game), Ipswich Town and Crystal Palace.

TEAM OF BAGGIES!

Over the years, a complete team of 11 players has been associated with both the Cherries and West Bromwich Albion and, lining up in a 3-3-4 formation, we have: Vince Bartram; Warren Cummings, Billy Gripton, Liam Ridgewell, Meynell Burgin, Billy Lunn, David Smith, Wayne Fereday, Billy Elliott, Luther Blissett, Carl Heggs. Substitute: Andy W. Smith. Freddie Cox and Tony Pulis would be joint managers, Richard O'Kelly an assistant and Gerry Peyton the goalkeeping coach

MILESTONE AGAINST THE CHERRIES

Jordan Rhodes's goal against Bournemouth in August 2014 was Blackburn Rovers' 7,000th in the Football League, in their 4,584th game.

EXTENDED CAREER

Journeyman Steve Claridge had a wonderful playing career which spanned 30 years (1982–2012). In this time he served with no less than 23 different clubs, 16 of them being members of the Football League when joining. Born in Portsmouth in 1966, Claridge started off as a youth team player at Fratton Park and went on to assist, in turn, the following clubs: Fareham Town, Bournemouth (November 1984–October 1985), Weymouth, Basingstoke Town, Crystal Palace, Aldershot, Cambridge United, Luton Town, Cambridge United (again), Birmingham City, Leicester City (signed for £1.2m in March 1996), Portsmouth (as a player, then player-manager), Wolverhampton Wanderers, Millwall, Weymouth (for a second time, as player-manager), Brighton & Hove Albion, Brentford, Wycombe Wanderers, Millwall (again, as player-manager), Gillingham, Walsall, Bournemouth (for a second spell, December 2006), Worthing, AFC Wimbledon, Harrow Borough, Weymouth (for a third spell) and finally Gosport Borough, retiring in the summer of 2012. He won the Third Division championship with Cambridge in 1991, the Second Division title and the Leyland DAF Trophy with Birmingham in 1995, and the League Cup with Leicester in 1997 (his extra-time goal beating Middlesbrough). He also netted a dramatic 120th-minute winner against his former club Crystal Palace in the 1996 play-off final at Wembley which shot the Foxes into the Premier League. The scorer of 298 goals in 976 club matches (at various levels), his Football League record was also mighty impressive: 194 goals in 641 appearances. And his senior record, not including non-league action, realised 223 goals in 765 games. He netted just once in nine outings for the Cherries. Striker Iyseden Christie played for 17 different clubs between 1995 and 2014, including Coventry City, Bournemouth (four games on loan in 1996), Mansfield Town, Leyton Orient, Rochdale, Kidderminster Harriers, Stevenage and Torquay United. George Best also assisted 17 clubs during his 21-year career from 1963–84. These included Manchester United, Stockport County, Fulham, Bournemouth (five appearances in 1983), Hibernian, Los Angeles Aztecs, San Jose Earthquakes and Fort Lauderdale Strikers. Phil Ashworth played for 16 clubs from the late 1960s to the mid-1980s, including Blackburn Rovers, Bournemouth (31 league outings in 1975/76), Portsmouth, Rochdale, Scunthorpe United, Southport and Workington. Another 16-club man was Leslie Roberts, born in the Black Country in 1901, who scored 10 goals in 51 league games for the Cherries in the mid-1920s. His other employers included Crystal Palace and Manchester City. Inside-forward Tommy Anderson also served with 16 clubs between 1955 and 1968 in England, Scotland, Ireland, Wales and Australia. He made five appearances for the Cherries in 1958. Reg Keating, born near Leeds in 1904, played for 16 clubs including Birmingham, Bournemouth (1936/37), Cardiff City, Carlisle United, Doncaster Rovers and Norwich City. He had his best years with Cardiff (35 goals in 70 league games) while his Bournemouth record was five goals in 11 league outings. England schoolboy goalkeeper Phil Kite served with 14 different clubs between 1980 and 1996, including both from Bristol. He was with Bournemouth in 1989/90 (seven league games played) and was on loan to half of the clubs he served. Kevin Russell, born in Portsmouth in 1966, made 456 league appearances with 12 clubs: Brighton & Hove Albion, Portsmouth, Wrexham, Leicester City, Peterborough United, Cardiff City, Hereford United, Stoke City, Burnley, Bournemouth (1994/95), Notts County and Wrexham. Another 12-club man was forward Dave Regis whose nine-year career (1989–98) took him to Barnet, Barnsley, Birmingham City, Bournemouth (six appearances in 1992), Leyton Orient, Lincoln City, Notts County, Peterborough United, Plymouth Argyle, Scunthorpe United, Southend United and Stoke City. Another nomadic footballer was midfielder Jimmy Case who played for 11 different clubs during his career – South Liverpool, Liverpool, Southampton, Bournemouth (July 1991–July 1992), Halifax Town, Wrexham, Darlington, British Wanneroo (Australia), Darlington, Brighton & Hove Albion, Sittingbourne and Brighton & Hove Albion again, as player-manager. Capped once by England at Under-23 level, Case retired in November 1995 with 626 league appearances to his credit,

40 for the Cherries. He also managed Bashley for two seasons. As a player Case helped Liverpool win four league titles, three European Cups, the UEFA Cup, the European Super Cup, the League Cup and the FA Charity Shield on four occasions.

WILLIAMS X 4

Over a period of 15 years, between 1981 and 1996, Bournemouth were served by four players named Williams: David (1992/93), Gareth (1994–96), John (1986–91) and Keith (1981–87). David made 412 league appearances during his career which also took him to Bristol Rovers and Norwich City. John made 117 appearances for the Cherries and Keith 102.

LONG SERVICE

Dickie Dowsett played for Bournemouth from June 1957 until November 1962 and, after retiring in the mid-1960s, he returned to Dean Court and served as the club's commercial manager from 1968 until 1983; 20 years in total, making him one of the Cherries' longest serving employees (See under: Dowsett – Top Man). Steve Fletcher was also associated with Bournemouth for over 20 years – two spells as a player, 1992–2007 and 2009–13 – and thereafter as a scout. He is now the club's official ambassador.

GLASS CUTS IT FINE

Goalkeeper Jimmy Glass made over 100 first-class appearances for Bournemouth in two seasons, 1996–98. He was then transferred to Swindon Town and, towards the end of the 1998/99 season, he was loaned out to Carlisle United in an emergency. At the time, the Cumbrians were battling against relegation to the Conference, along with Scarborough, and they knew they had to win their final game of the season, at home to Plymouth Argyle on 8 May 1999, to stand any chance of retaining their Football League status. Carlisle were propping up the table on 46 points, one less than Scarborough who were at home to Peterborough United. It was a nervous afternoon and, with radios to the ears of hundreds of supporters, the score from the McCain Stadium was always known. As it was, Scarborough's game ended in a draw and actually finished a couple of minutes before Carlisle's. The Boro fans were celebrating on the pitch thinking their team had done enough to stay up. 141 miles away on the edge of the Lake District, Carlisle were fearing the worst. With time fast running out they were being held 1–1 by Argyle. Then, with barely ten seconds remaining, Glass went up for a corner and when the ball came over, he volleyed home the winning goal after the visiting keeper had parried Scott Dobie's forceful header. There was sheer delight around Brunton

Park and Glass was carried off the pitch, shoulder high, by the delighted Carlisle fans in the best-of-season crowd of 7,599. Commenting for Radio Cumbria, Derek Lacey described that late drama as follows, 'Everyone is in the Plymouth half of the field, including United's goalkeeper. The corner kick comes in; Dobie gets in a header, Plymouth's keeper punches the ball away...goal...Oh, Jimmy Glass! Jimmy Glass, the goalkeeper has scored! There's a pitch invasion...there is a pitch invasion... the referee has been swamped... they're bouncing on the crossbar... United are safe. What a finish, amazing.' Glass, who still vividly recalls that memorable occasion today, retired as a full-time professional footballer at the age of 27 to become an IT salesman. But he still turned out for various non-league clubs for another four years. He now lives in the picturesque Dorset village of Lytchett Matravers with his wife Louise and their twins, and runs a taxi business in the nearby town of Wimbourne Minster. In a 2013 BBC interview Glass stated, 'It is quite tough because some go on to fame and fortune, and some go on to driving a cab and living a normal life like me. It is quite difficult to understand your place in life from being this guy who will never be forgotten to being the guy worrying about your next bill. The goal was an amazing part of my life and is there to be enjoyed. Someone on Saturday will be a hero and someone will be a villain. It is an incredible feeling.' For the record, Glass was born near the Epsom race course in Surrey in August 1973 and was a youth team player with Chelsea before joining Crystal Palace. He went on to play, in turn, for Portsmouth, Gillingham, Burnley, the Cherries, Swindon Town, Carlisle (loan), Cambridge United, Brentford, Oxford United, Crawley Town, Brockenhurst (loan), Kingstonian, Lewes and finally Weymouth. He made almost 300 club appearances at various levels, including 215 in the league (1989–2004) and he scored one goal – which will always be remembered in Carlisle. In October 2011, Glass joined Poole Town as the club's goalkeeping coach, working on a voluntary basis.

THEY CAME BACK

Six players – Patrick (Patsy) Gallacher, Jack Kirkham, Fred Marsden, Tommy Paton, Joe Sanaghan and Bill Tunnicliffe – all appeared in competitive games for Bournemouth before, during and after World War Two. Inside-forward Gallacher, born in Glasgow in 1913, played for Third Lanark and Blackburn before making 35 league appearances for the Cherries from June 1938–May 1947. Kirkham, from Ellesmere Port in Cheshire (born in 1918), was a utility forward who struck 26 in 47 for the Cherries whom he served from October 1938 until May 1947. Marsden, born in Blackburn in 1911, played full-back for Accrington Stanley and Wolves prior to making over 200 appearances for Bournemouth, 194 in the league, between May 1936 and June 1949. Wing-half Paton was born in Saltcoats in 1918 and he too played for Wolves, albeit as a reserve, and Swansea Town before netting eight goals in 46 Third Division South games for Bournemouth from February 1939 to January 1948. He moved to Watford and went on to make over 200 club appearances during his career. Sanaghan was a full-back, born in Motherwell in 1914, who assisted Bradford Park Avenue and Stockport County either side of his spell at Dean Court – June 1937 to August 1949. He made 170 league appearances for the Cherries and 227 in his career. Tunnicliffe, born in Stoke-on-Trent in 1920, was an outside-left who played for Port Vale before spending nine years with Bournemouth from May 1938 to June 1947. He scored seven goals in 49 league games before transferring to Wrexham. He later assisted Bradford City.

INTO MANAGEMENT

Over the years many former Bournemouth players entered into management (some even did it while still kicking a ball). Here are some of the ex-Cherries who took charge of football clubs (other than the Cherries) after 1945: Tommy Anderson (Limerick), David Armstrong (Waterlooville), Kevin Bond, Brian Chambers (Poole Town), Steve Claridge (Millwall), Steve Cotterill (Bristol City and Portsmouth), Fred Davies (Shrewsbury Town, Merthyr Tydfil, Weymouth), Jamie Day (Welling United, Ebbsfleet United), Warren Feeney (Linfield), Don Givens (Xamax/Switzerland, also the Republic of Ireland), Ivan Golac (Partizan Belgrade, Torquay United, Dundee United, IA Akranes, Sartid Smederevo and FC Karpaty Lviv), Joe Harvey (Barrow, Workington and Newcastle United), John Impey (Weymouth, Torquay United and Totnes Town), David James (player-manager, Kerala Blasters), Dave Madden (Cork Athletic), Trevor Morgan (Sorrento FC, Sarawak FA, Sengkang Punggol, East Bengal, Dempo SC), Paul Morrell (Poole Town), Mark Morris (Dorchester Town), Harry Redknapp (West Ham United, Portsmouth, Southampton, Tottenham Hotspur and Queens Park Rangers), John Rudge (Port Vale), Shaun Teale (Burscough and Northwich Victoria), Train (caretaker, Walsall) and Jack Whitehouse (Worcester City). Bill Voisey bossed Millwall during World War Two.

NOTES ON THE BOSSES

Rudge was in charge at Vale Park for 16 years, from 1983–99, twice taking the Potteries club to Wembley. As a player he served with Huddersfield Town, Carlisle United, Torquay United, Bristol Rovers and Bournemouth, scoring twice in 21 league games for the Cherries (1975–77). Cotterill led Bristol City to the League 1 title in 2014/15. Voisey also managed the Great Britain Olympic soccer team in 1936. Former Cherries star Stephen

Purches was appointed as the club's development squad manager in 2013, while ex-player Carl Fletcher became the club's youth team manager.

BASHLEY FOOTBALL CLUB

Formed in 1947, Bashley are a non-league football club based in New Milton, a village on the outskirts of Bournemouth. Over the years several top players, some who have links with the Cherries, have been associated with the Bash and they include: Stuart Barfoot, Neal Bartlett, Wayne Brown, Robbie Carroll, Jimmy Case (one of the better-known stars), John Chiedozie, Paul Compton, Aaron Cook, Max Cream, Wade Elliott, Justin Keeler, Ian Leigh, Richie Moran, Jake Newton, Brian O'Donnell, Alex Parsons, Stuart Ritchie, Jordan Rose, Dan Strugnell and David West.

FLURRY OF GOALS

Between Boxing Day 1997 and 10 January 1998, Bournemouth played three league games which produced scorelines of 4-0, 3-5 and 3-0 – 15 goals in 270 minutes. The Cherries also played out successive 3-3 draws v. Gillingham and Leeds United in October and November 1998, and against Blackburn Rovers and Cardiff City in rounds two and three of the League Cup in 2004.

OUSTED BY THE TYKES

In the 1998/99 season, Bournemouth were knocked out of the League Cup (2-1) and the FA Cup (3-1) by Barnsley, each time at Oakwell.

REGULAR SCORERS

Between late October 2000 and early May 2001, Bournemouth scored in 34 consecutive games (31 in the league and three in the FA Cup), a club record. The Cherries netted 70 or more league goals in each campaign over a period of seven years from 1925–32. Their final total was 523 in 294 games, with 84 coming in 1928/29. In three seasons, 1956–59, Bournemouth scored 238 league goals. They also bagged 23 in nine FA Cup ties.

FOREIGN BODIES

Over the years, Bournemouth have been served by quite a few players who were born outside the UK (overseas) with some of them taking British citizenship. Among them we have the following: Diogo Andrade (born Lisbon, Portugal), Christian Atsu (Ada Foah, Ghana), Mathieu Baudry (Le Havre, France), Asmir Begovic (Bosnia-Herzegovinia), George Bellis (Khadki, India), Artur Boruc (Poland), Dimitris Brinias (Australia), Benjamin Buchel (Liechenstein), Dave Chadwick (India), Jean-Francoise Christophe (France), Mohamed Coulibaly (Switzerland), Ian Cox (Trinidad & Tobago), Lauri Dalla Valle (Finland), Lorenzo Davids (Suriname), Franck Demouge (Netherlands), Efan Ekoku (Nigeria), Amos Foyewa (Nigeria), Max Gradel (Ivory Coast), Adam Griffiths (Sydney, Australia), Brent Goulet (USA), Scott Guyett (Australia), Zavan Hines (Jamaica), Willie Huck (France), Shwan Jalal (Baghdad, Iraq), Kenwyne Jones (Trinidad & Tobago), Claus Jorgensen (Faroe Islands), Tresor Kandol (Banga, Zaire/DR Congo), Jem Karacan (Turkey), Yann Kermorgant (Vannes, France), Jo Kuffour (Ghana), Scott McDonald (Dandenong, Australia), Michael Menetrier (France), Dudley Milligan (South Africa), Emmanuel Omoyinmi (Nigeria), Francisco Peed (Argentina), Jamie Peters (Canada), Tokelo Rantie (Free State, South Africa), Carroll Lloyd Richards (Jamaica), Dani/Ferreira Rodrigues Daniel (Madeira, Portugal), Franck Rolling (France), Fawzi Saadi (Algeria), Yazalde Damas Santos (USA), Ricky Sappleton (Jamaica), Elhadjit Seydi (Dakar, Senegal), Frank Simec (Missouri, USA), Frank Songo'o (Cameroon), Brian Statham (Zimbabwe), Marek Stech (Czech Republic), Mark Stein (South Africa), Nelson Stiffle (British Raj, India), Andrew Surman (South Africa), Chris Tardif (Guernsey), Lyle Taylor (Montserrat), Jo Tessem (Orlandet, Norway), Pascali Tetu (France), Jake Thomas (Trinidad & Tobago), Bjarne Vidarsson (Iceland), Arnold Woollard (Bermuda), Chris Wreh (Liberia), Stephane Zubar (Guadeloupe). Some lists have Londoner Leslie Parodi (a 1970s Cherry) as being born in the USA.

LOCAL TALENT

Bournemouth have signed several players who were born within walking distance, even a bus journey or ferry ride away from the club. Not including those from the areas of nearby Portsmouth and Southampton, they include, in A-Z order: Kevin Allen (born, Isle of Wight), Kieron Baker (Isle of Wight), Brian Benjafield (Barton-on-Sea), Dave Bewley (Bournemouth), Lee Bradbury (Isle of Wight), Martin Bridge (Hartley Whitney), Keith Brown (Bournemouth), Derek Burns (Bournemouth), Roy Burns (Bournemouth), Dennis Bushby (Poole), Josh Carmichael (Poole), Micky Cave (Weymouth), Paul Christopher (Poole), Billy Clark (Christchurch), David Coleman (Salisbury), Shaun Cooper (Isle of Wight), Harry Cornick (Poole), James Coutts (Weymouth), Michael Dean (Weymouth), Jack Dixon (Bournemouth), Billy Elliott (Poole), Matt Finlay (Salisbury), Chris Foote (Bournemouth), Peter Gledstone (Christchurch), Howard Goddard (Over

Wallop), Anthony Griffiths (Bournemouth), Stephen Gritt (Bournemouth), Tony Gulliver (Salisbury), Horace F. Harrison (Bournemouth), James Hayter (Isle of Wight), Bill Heath (Bournemouth), Paddy Hester (Poole), Danny Ings (Winchester), Stuart Kearn (Bournemouth), Morgan Lewis (Bournemouth), Roy Littlejohn (Bournemouth), Dennis Longhorn (Hythe), Jake McCarthy (Blandford), Norman McKay (Poole), Harry Maidment (Bournemouth), Ken Marshall (Bournemouth), Harry Meyer (Christchurch), Billy Miles (Bournemouth), Paul Mitchell (Bournemouth), Paul Morrell (Poole), Neil Moss (New Milton), Mark Nightingale (Salisbury), Marcus Oldbury (Bournemouth), Mark Omerod (Bournemouth), Harry Baven Penton (Bournemouth), Russell Perrett (Barton-on-Sea), Ernest Phillipson-Masters (Bournemouth), Brett Pitman (Jersey), Carl Preston (Poole), Ryan Price (Bournemouth), Jamie Redknapp (Barton-on-Sea), James Reeve (Weymouth), Derek Reeves (Poole), Kevin Reeves (Burley, Hants), Paul Rideout (Bournemouth), Bob Saunders (Poole), Chris Shaw (Bournemouth), Eric Seymour Sibley (Christchurch), Chris Shaw (Bournemouth), David Simmons (Isle of Wight), Harvey Sinclair (Bournemouth), Bob Smith (Bournemouth), Nigel Spackman (Romsey), Brian Stock (Winchester), Jayden Stockley (Poole), Derek Stroud (Wimbourne), Dan Strugnell (Christchurch), Alan Summerhill (Liss), Jack Sutton (Bournemouth), Harold Tarrant (Bournemouth), Rod Taylor (Wimbourne), Dan Thomas (Poole), John Thomas (Poole), Phil Thomas (Sherbourne), Ron Tilsed (Weymouth), David Town (Bournemouth), Matt Tubbs (Salisbury), Sam Vokes (Lymington), Christer Warren (Poole), George Webb (Poole), Jamie Whisken (Bournemouth), Jimmy White (Parkstone), Kevin White (Poole), Brian Wood (Poole), Bob Young (Bournemouth) and Cecil Young (Bournemouth). And perhaps we could add Howard Goddard who was born in Over Wallop. Rod Belfitt, a teenage trialist at Dean Court who went on to do well with Leeds United, was born in Bournemouth. In 2009/10, three players from Poole all turned out for Bournemouth's first team: Jayden Stockley, Dan Thomas and George Webb. Welsh international Sam Vokes attended Brockenhurst College.

BUSY SEASONS

Bournemouth completed 59 competitive games in 1983/84; 46 league matches, seven FA Cup and League Cup ties, and six in the Associate Members Cup which they won. A total of 53 competitive games were played by the Cherries in 2014/15 (46 league).

SEMI-FINAL DESPAIR

After knocking out Oxford United (3-2), Leyton Orient (1-0) and Cardiff City (2-1), Bournemouth were defeated by Bristol City in the semi-final of the LDV Vans Trophy in 2002/03. Despite taking a 15th-minute lead through Carl Fletcher, they went down 3-1 at Dean Court in front of 5,125 fans. The Cherries also lost to Brentford on penalties in the semi-final of the Freight Rover Trophy competition in 1984/85.

THE 'BEST' FOOTBALLER!

Northern Ireland international George Best spent most of his career with Manchester United, for whom he scored 179 goals in 470 appearances, but in March and April 1983, as a loanee, he turned out in five league games for the Cherries. Voted the European Footballer of the Year and FWA Footballer of the Year in 1968 when he helped United win the European Cup, he was described by many as the greatest footballer to grace the game, certainly since the World War Two. Born in Belfast on 22 May 1946, 'Bestie' was a terrific dribbler who teased and tormented defenders for over 20 years. His playing style combined pace, skill, balance, feints, two-footedness, goalscoring and the ability to beat opponents. Best surprisingly quit Old Trafford in 1974 at age 27, but later returned to the game and played for several other clubs including Stockport County, Fulham and, of course, the Cherries, before retiring in 1984, age 38. On the international front, he scored nine times in 37 outings for his country (1964–77), but never displayed his skills in the finals of a European Championship or World Cup. Such was his enormous talent and indeed his charisma, that he became one of the first celebrity footballers, earning the nickname 'El Beatle' but his subsequent extravagant lifestyle led to various problems, most notably alcoholism, which he suffered from for the rest of his life. After leaving football, he spent some time as a pundit, opened a boutique and also a bar in London, but financial and health problems ruined his life. He died in 2005, age 59, due to complications from the immunosuppressive drugs he needed to take after being controversially granted an NHS liver transplant in 2002. Before he passed away, Best was voted 16th in the IFFHS World Player of the Century election in 1999 and was one of the inaugural 22 inductees into the English Football Hall of Fame three years later. In 2004 he was also voted 19th in the public UEFA Golden Jubilee Poll and was named in the FIFA 100 list of the world's greatest living players. Three-time Brazilian World Cup winner Pelé said, 'George Best was the greatest footballer in the world – an unbelievable player.' And later Best himself was quoted as saying, 'Pelé called me the greatest footballer in the world. That is the ultimate salute to my life.' After his death, on what would have been his 60th birthday, Belfast City Airport was renamed the George Best Belfast City Airport. Best's career realised 709 club appearances and 253 goals.

BIG WINS

The Cherries scored 12 goals in two home league games in 2003/04, whipping Luton Town 6-3 and Wrexham 6-0. In contrast they lost 5-1 at Tranmere.

CHERRIES LEGEND

Without doubt Steve Fletcher is a true Bournemouth legend who holds the club record for the most senior appearances. Born in Hartlepool on 26 July 1972, he began his professional career with his hometown club and made his league debut as an 18-year-old in 1990. He moved the 334 miles south to Bournemouth for what would turn out to be a bargain fee of just £30,000 in July 1992. Spending the next 15 years with the Cherries, he played in more than 600 first-class games and struck over 100 goals. Released by his then manager Kevin Bond at the end of the 2006/07 season, he subsequently joined recently relegated League 2 side Chesterfield where he stayed until May 2008, turning down a contract renewal with the Spireites due to family commitments. In the summer of 2008, he signed for Crawley Town on a free transfer, agreeing an initial one-year contract. Eight months later, however, 'Fletch' returned to Dean Court on a short-term contract until the end of the season, being given the option to extend it for another term after that. He made his 500th league appearance (600th first team appearance overall) for the Cherries early in the 2009/10 season and, in the April of 2010, the club renamed the North Stand at Dean Court after him. Two months later, with everyone rejoicing on and off the pitch, Fletcher – to the delight of the supporters – signed a one-year contract extension as the Cherries celebrated promotion to League 1. Appointed assistant manager to Lee Bradbury in January 2011 (after Eddie Howe had left the club to manage Burnley), 'Fletch' scored his 100th league goal for Bournemouth in a 3-3 draw at Peterborough United on 1 April 2011. Bournemouth qualified for the play-offs that season, but lost on penalties in the two-legged semi-final against Huddersfield Town. Fletcher resigned as the Cherries' assistant manager in November 2011, saying that it would be more beneficial for the team and the club if he focused on playing for the remainder of his contract. Having been restricted to brief substitute appearances since resigning as Bradbury's assistant, Fletcher was loaned out to Plymouth Argyle in March 2012, but was told that he was still part of the manager's plans. By coincidence his boss at Home Park was his former Bournemouth team-mate Carl Fletcher, who had been in charge of the Pilgrims since September 2011. Carl and 'Fletch' are close friends and go back years. And Fletcher admitted that Plymouth was the only club he contemplated going to, simply because Carl was manager. 'If it hadn't been for him, I wouldn't have even thought about moving to Devon,' he said. Fletcher made his debut for the Pilgrims in a 1-0 win over Bradford City on 31 March and appeared in five more matches, helping the club secure their future in League 2 after a turbulent season. Following Argyle's 2-2 draw at Morecambe, Fletcher was recalled by Bournemouth's then caretaker manager Paul Groves ahead of the final league match of the campaign, and with promotion confirmed the Dean Court legend officially announced his retirement as a player, saying, 'I felt the time was right to hang up my boots and seek another role within the club.' Shortly after his career had ended, it was revealed that newly promoted Conference South side Gosport Borough had asked about his availability. In June 2013 it was announced that Fletcher would stay at Bournemouth as a senior scout and, nine months later, in March 2014, he was honoured with the Sir Tom Finney Award by the Football League. Steve Fletcher's playing career covered 23 years during which time he netted 136 goals in 834 club games, including 121 in 727 games for the Cherries. Wonderful stats for a great player. Jack Howe, Fletcher's grandfather (born in 1915, died in 1987), played competitive football for Hartlepool United, Derby County and Huddersfield Town between 1934 and 1951, making 276 league appearances and scoring three goals as a full-back. He was also capped three times by England at senior level.

BAD AWAY DAYS

Bournemouth conceded no less than 11 goals in two successive away games in August 2013, losing 6-1 at Watford and 5-1 at Huddersfield. Surprisingly the Cherries let in only 16 more goals on their travels that season, which saw them finish tenth in the Championship, six points off the play-offs.

GREAT FIGHTBACK

In October 2013, Bournemouth's players and travelling supporters feared the worst when they conceded two goals in the first ten minutes of their away league game at Millwall. Slowly but surely though, the Cherries clawed their way back into the game and reduced the deficit two minutes before half-time through Ryan Fraser. After what appeared to be a stern pep-talk in the dressing room, the second half was a completely different story. In fact, it was virtually one-way traffic towards the Lions' goal as the home side completely lost their roar, and rampant Bournemouth stormed to an emphatic 5-2 victory with further goals from Steve Cook (50 minutes), Harry Arter (55), a Lewis Grabban penalty (59) and Brett Pitman's late spot-kick (90).

BLITZED BY THE SHRIMPERS

Bournemouth travelled to the seaside resort of Morecambe for a league game on 12 December 2009, but it turned out to be a horrible experience for Eddie Howe's team as the home side romped to a 5-0 win at Christie Park in front of just 2,034 fans. This was Morecambe's biggest win since they entered the Football League in 2007 and remained so until they defeated Crawley Town 6-0 in September 2011.

A LOT OF PLAYERS!

Players used by Bournemouth in league games during a season: 39 in 2011/12 (16 scored), 37 in 2008/09, 36 in 2006/07 and 2007/08; 34 in 1994/95, 1995/96 and 1999/2000; 33 in 1994/95 and 1995/96, and 32 in 2012/13 (15 scored).

CLUB CHAIRMEN

Here are the men who have served AFC Bournemouth as chairman since 1969. The years in given are approximate, according to when the club's AGM took place: H.G. Walker, LL.B (1969–82); R.J.C. Barton (1983–88); J.P. Nolan (1988–90); P.W. Hayward, JP (1990/91); N. Hayward (1991–94); K. Gardiner (1994–96); T.S. Watkins (1997–2000); A.S. Waisland (2000–02); P.I. Phillips (2002–06); J. Mostyn (2006–09); E. Mitchell/Maxim Demin, jointly (2011–13); E. Mitchell/Neill Blake (2013/14); J. Mostyn (2014/15).

APRIL FOOLS

Bournemouth were well beaten 3-0 by Leeds United in a Second Division game at Elland Rod on 1 April 1989. Carl Shutt made the Cherries look rather foolish with a hat-trick in front of 21,095 fans. The Cherries have won on April Fool's Day, beating Leyton Orient 2-0 in 1995 and Scunthorpe United in 2013, Brett Pitman scoring in the 11th minute of the latter game. They also shared six goals in a thrilling league match with Peterborough United on 1 April 2011.

PORTSMOUTH LINK

Joe Armstrong, Percy Cherrett, Hugh Davey, John Friar, Arthur Keeley, Billy Lee (also with Bournemouth Athletic and Bournemouth Wanderers), George Marshall, Bob Mortimore, Herbert Powell (with Boscombe), Ron Ranson, Jack Smith, Jack Surtees, Eden Taylor and Len Williams are among the players who served with both the Cherries and Pompey

before the World War Two. However, after the hostilities, the number of footballers who have chose to wear the blue of Pompey and the colours of Bournemouth increased tenfold and they include: Darren Anderton, Phil Ashworth, Warren Aspinall, David Best, David Birmingham, Lee Bradbury, Chris Burns, Lewis Buxton, Tommy Casey, Colin Clarke, Steve Claridge, Shaun Cooper, Martin Crainie, Reg Cutler, Dani (Ferreira Rodrigues Daniel), Ian Drummond, Keith East, Wes Fogden, Jimmy Glass, Ivan Golac, Dennis Hall, Eddie Howe, Richard Hughes, Ralph Hunt, Richard Hughes, David James, Roger Jones, James Keene, George Lawrence, Steve Lovell, Martin MacDonald, Barry Mansell, Nicky Morgan, Gordon Neave, Marcus Painter, Jason Pearce, Tony Priscott, Billy Rafferty, Micky Reid, Matt Ritchie, Kevin Russell, Lee Russell, Derek Showers, Chris Tardif, Rod Taylor, Thomas Taylor, Rees Thomas, Wes Thomas, Bill (Willie) Thompson, Ron Tilsed, Matt Tubbs, Jamie Vincent, Joel Ward, James (Jimmy) White, Tom Williams, Marc Wilson and Paul Wood. Three men – Tony Pulis, Freddie Cox and Harry Redknapp – have managed both clubs, while ex-Pompey star Reg Flewin bossed Bournemouth and former Cherry Steve Cotterill likewise Pompey. Luther Blissett and Martin O'Connor both played for the Cherries, and were engaged as coaches at Portsmouth. Scottish international Richard Hughes was born in Glasgow in 1979, and actually started his playing career as a youth team player in Italy with Atalanta and then moved to Arsenal before joining the Cherries in 1998.

GOAL DROUGHT

Bournemouth failed to score in 20 of their 46 league games in 1995/96. They finished 14th in the table. They managed only two goals in eight matches during February and March. In 1996/97, the Cherries scored more than two goals in a game just twice – beating Luton Town 3-2 and Chesterfield 3-0, both at home. They finished 16th in the division.

OWN GOAL TREBLE

Former Bournemouth defender Jackie Randle holds a unique record – he is the only footballer ever to score a hat-trick of own goals in the same match. In September 1926, when playing left-back for Coventry City away at Bristol City, he netted three times past his own goalkeeper Jack Newton as the Sky Blues went down 3-0 in front of 12,000 fans at Ashton Gate. He made 11 appearances for the Cherries in 1933/34 and also played for Birmingham. He died in Bournemouth in 1990 at the ripe old age of 88.

DOUBLE IRISH – NOT DUTCH

With Bournemouth from 2012–14, Eunan O'Kane was born in Derry in July 1990 and played for Northern Ireland at Under-16, Under-17, Under-19, Under-20 and Under-21 levels before going on to star for the Republic of Ireland's Under-21 team. He was signed by the Cherries from Torquay United, having previously served with Everton and Coleraine.

NAP HAND

Having scored only five times in their 11 previous league games before taking on Blackpool at Dean Court in January 1993, the Cherries went goal crazy against the Seasiders, winning 5-1, but there were only 3,807 hardy supporters there to see the action.

SOLID DEFENCE

Bournemouth's resolute defence conceded only 30 goals in 46 league games in 1981/82 when they finished fourth in the Fourth Division (eight points behind champions Sheffield United) to gain promotion. The team also drew a record 19 games that season (11 at home, eight away). And, in fact, the Cherries lost only one league game during the second half of the campaign, 1-0 at Northampton in February. They won 12 and drew ten of 22 matches played, and in truth, that exceptionally high tally of draws stopped them from becoming champions themselves.

JOY OF PROMOTION AND RELEGATION DESPAIR

The first time Bournemouth actually gained promotion was in the summer of 1923, leaving the Southern League after gaining membership to the Football League's Third Division South. Since then, the Cherries have risen from a lower division into a higher one seven times: in 1970/71 (from the Fourth Division as runners-up); in 1981/82 (again from the Fourth Division with a fourth-place finish); in 1986/87 (from the Third Division as champions); in 2002/03 (from the Third Division for a third time, winning the play-off final after finishing fourth in the table); in 2009/10 (from League 2 as runners-up); in 2012/13 (as runners-up in League 1) and in 2014/15 (as Championship winners, rising into the division of dreams – the Premier League. In contrast, the Cherries have fallen from a higher tree on five occasions: in 1969/70 (down from the Third Division); in 1981/82 (relegated from the Third Division); in 1989/90 (from the Second Division); in 2001/02 (from the Second Division) and in 2008/09 (from League 2 following a ten-point deduction). The Cherries finished runners-up in the Third Division South in 1947/48, but in those days only one team (the champions) were promoted.

GOAL FAMINE

The Cherries failed to score in 20 of their 46 league games in 1995/96 when they finished 14th in the table. They managed only two goals in eight games during February and March.

GOAL MACHINES

Ted MacDougall scored a club record 49 goals for the Cherries in 1970/71; 42 in the Third Division (six penalties) and seven in the FA Cup. He actually topped the country's scoring charts, finishing ahead of Tony Brown (30 for WBA, Malcolm Macdonald (30 for Luton Town) and David Gwyther (27 for Swansea). The following season he struck another 47 (35 league, two League Cup and ten FA Cup), having previously notched 23 in 46 outings in 1969/70, making it a grand total of 119 for the club in just three campaigns. His overall record for the Cherries, before he left for Manchester United in September 1972, was an impressive 126 goals in 165 appearances. 'Super Ted' was also the first player to top the scoring charts in three different divisions; twice with Bournemouth in 1970/71 (Fourth Division) with 42 goals and in 1971/72 (Third Division) with 35 goals, and then with Norwich City in 1975/76 (Second Division) with 23 goals. Ron Eyre, a star between the two world wars, holds the club record for most league goals scored for the club in total aggregate, bagging 202 over a period of 11 years, from 1924–35. Eyre's tally of 27 in 1925/26 was three times more than any other Bournemouth player. In all the prolific Eyre, formerly of Sheffield Wednesday, netted 259 goals in 367 appearances in all competitions for the Cherries, ending up as the club's leading marksmen on four occasions, with totals of 27 in 1925/26, 29 in 1926/27, 30 in 1927/28 and 31 in 1928/29. In 2009/10, Brett Pittman scored 26 League 2 goals for the Cherries – the highest tally achieved at this level since MacDougall's haul of 35 in 1971/72. Over the years the Cherries – like every club in the country – have had some supreme goalscorers and here below are a few more who bulged the back of the nets during their respective careers (worldwide), not only for Bournemouth I might add. The total goals scored by each player is indicated in the brackets: Paul Aimson (141), Brian Bedford (229), George Best (147), Bert Bliss (112), Luther Blissett (215), Phil Boyer (159), Steve Claridge (194), Brian Clark (217), Colin Clarke (134), Jamie Cureton (240*), Jermain Defoe (167*), Dicky Dowsett (106), Efan Ekoku (109), Steve Fletcher (112), James Hayter (152*), Jack Howarth (190), Ralph Hunt (184), Steve Lovell (141), Stan Newsham (118), Jimmy Quinn (210), Billy Rafferty (145), Derek Reeves (153), Kevin Reeves (103), Paul Rideout (147), John O'Rourke (165), Mark Stein (201) and Billy Tunnicliffe (102). * Still adding to total in 2015.

MAC AND PHIL

During their playing careers at club level, Ted MacDougall and Phil Boyer, as strike partners in the same front line, scored a total of 195 goals while serving with York City (1968/69), Bournemouth (1970–72), Norwich City (1974/75) and Southampton (1977/78). 'Supermac' netted 127 and Boyer 68.

ON LOAN

One of the early players – possibly the first – signed on loan by Bournemouth was Alec Bugg from Ipswich Town in February 1970. A goalkeeper, he appeared in four league games towards the end of that season. The first outfield loanee recruited by Bournemouth was Pat Holland from West Ham United. Signed in March 1971, he made ten League appearances for the Cherries during the last two months of that season before returning to Upton Park. In season 2014/15, the Cherries loaned out three players to Coventry City – Ryan Allsop, Mohamed Coulibaly and Josh McQuoid. And they helped keep the Sky Blues in League 1.

BEST PROGRAMME

Bournemouth's official matchday programme was voted the best in the Championship for 2014/15, beating 23 other clubs for the top award. Fulham's publication was second, followed, in turn, by those produced by Norwich City, Reading, Wolves and Brighton & Hove Albion. Around 3,000 copies of the highly-collectable programme are sold every home match.

AT HOME IN DORCHESTER

After beating Northampton Town 2-0 on Saturday 28 April 2001 in front of 6,511 fans, Bournemouth moved out of their Dean Court ground to set up a temporary base at Dorchester's Avenue Stadium. This was a simple solution while the club's new ground was being built, partially on the site of the old one, with the pitch being turned by 90 degrees. The 2001/02 season, however, proved to be a defining one for the Cherries in more ways than one. The temporary stay at Dorchester ended with a 4-2 league win over Notts County (after being 2-0 down) and soon afterwards, on 10 November, Bournemouth returned to the newly-named and built Fitness First Stadium, later renamed the Goldsands Stadium. Brian Stock, born in Winchester, scored the first goal at the new ground, netting in the 29th minute of a 3-0 victory over Wrexham. James Hayter and Jason Tindall struck the other two in front of a crowd of 5,031. The Cherries played nine league games on Dorchester's ground – winning six, drawing one and losing two, scoring 16 goals and conceding nine. After that venture, unfortunately, a young Bournemouth side found it tough going and, after a hard long slog, they were relegated with this rather dismal record:

Venue	P	W	D	L	F	A	Pts
Home	23	9	4	10	36	23	31
Away	23	1	10	12	20	38	13
Totals	46	10	14	22	56	61	44

In the dropzone at the start of March, and with 11 games still remaining, the Cherries struggled, winning only two more fixtures (5-1 against fellow relegation candidates Northampton Town and 3-1 v. Chesterfield). They knew they were down with two matches left, the final nail being hammered into the coffin at Wrexham on the last day of the season. Bournemouth had played Dorchester Town in the second round of the FA Cup in 1981/82. After a 1-1 draw at The Avenue Stadium, the Cherries won the replay 2-1. And in a friendly at Dorchester in mid-July 2014, the Cherries went goal crazy against their near neighbours, winning 11-0 with goals from Yann Kermorgant (4, one penalty), Matt Ritchie (2), Brett Pitman (2), Harry Arter, Callum Wilson and Ben Whitfield. It was 8-0 at half-time and manager Eddie Howe gave 23 players a taste of the action over the 90 minutes – the most used in any single first team game in the club's history.

DEVELOPMENT SQUAD

Bournemouth introduced a development squad for the start of the 2012/13 season, as part of the club's new academy plans, aiming to 'bridge the gap between the youth team set-up and the first team'. Former player Stephen Purches was named as the team manager/coach, and members of the first team squad regularly attend training and coaching sessions. Purches was subsequently upgraded to development squad manager in 2013. The squad played four friendlies in July 2014, beating Hamworthy 4-0, Wimbourne 4-0 and Sholing 3-2, but losing 2-0 against Poole Town.

MY SON

'Despite the fact that he is my son, I would always want him by my side whichever club I was with. His character and ability will stand the test of time.' Words spoken by the former Bournemouth manager John Bond when defending the signing of his son, Kevin, for Manchester City in March 1981. Three months later Kevin asked for a transfer!

THE AWARD-WINNING MATCH PROGRAMME ON SALE OUTSIDE THE GROUND

RECORD BREAKER

On New Year's Day 2001, striker Jermain Defoe broke a 74-year-old Bournemouth club record by scoring in his eighth consecutive game. He went on to find the net in ten matches overall, claiming 12 goals in total. Defoe ended the season as the Cherries' top marksman with 19 goals, seven more than James Hayter.

DEBUT BOY

Bournemouth's midfielder Matt Ritchie made his debut for Scotland against Northern Ireland in a friendly international in March 2015. And from his 85th-minute right-wing corner, substitute Christophe Berra rose highest to nod home the game's only goal of a rather dour encounter in front of 28,000 spectators inside Hampden Park. Three months later Ritchie netted his first international goal to earn the Scots a 1-0 friendly win over Qatar at Easter Road, Edinburgh.

WELSH TESTS

Bournemouth have played nine different Welsh clubs in competitive matches since 1923, and they are: Aberdare Athletic (eight games), Caernarfon Athletic (two), Cardiff City (43), Chester City (16), Lovells Athletic (two), Merthyr Town (15), Newport County (85), Swansea Town/City (53) and Wrexham (44). The Cherries' full record against the clubs from the Principality is fairly good. It reads: played 268, won 104, drawn 63 and lost 101. Their best figures are against Cardiff: 18 wins and 12 draws from 43 meetings. They have, however, suffered 36 defeats at the hands of Newport, 23 versus Swansea and 19 v. Wrexham.

THE OPPOSITION

Since 1923 Bournemouth have played against 155 different football clubs in major competitions (over 100 in the Football League). They have met most of the current 92 league teams, albeit some of them rarely, including Arsenal and Tottenham Hotspur once each, Everton three times and Chelsea five. They have played four teams over 100 times – Reading 111 (winning 44 and losing 42), Swindon Town 109 (41 wins and 39 defeats), Watford 107 (37 victories and 38 losses) and Brighton & Hove Albion 104 (38 won, 37 lost). The Cherries have also taken on Queens Park Rangers 74 times, Aldershot/Town 69, Crystal Palace 64, Norwich City 54, Swansea 53, and Blackpool and Hull City both 41. And they've opposed Liverpool on six occasions, Manchester City also six, Manchester United eight, and both Aston Villa and West Ham five. And for the record they've played

Weymouth twice, Yeovil 19 times. Probably the Cherries' worst record is against Leeds United: ten defeats in 13 games. They've lost five of their eight matches against Manchester United, four in the FA Cup (6-0, 2-1, 3-0 and 1-0) and one in the League Cup (2-0), and they've also been beaten on four occasions (in six games) by Liverpool, Manchester City and Sunderland.

NEAR NEIGHBOURS

The grounds of rivals Bournemouth and Portsmouth are 51.9 miles apart (via the M27) and so far they have met 20 times at competitive level, with Pompey having the better record as at May 2015 with nine wins to their name against Bournemouth's seven, with four games drawn. The first two league meetings took place in 1923/24 when both teams were in the Third Division. Pompey won 3-0 at Fratton Park before forcing a goalless draw at Dean Court. The next encounters, in 1961/62, saw Bournemouth draw 1-1 at Portsmouth and earn a 2-0 win at Dean Court to collect two Third Division points. Bournemouth knocked Pompey out of the League Cup in 1971/72, winning a first-round home tie 2-1, Ted MacDougall scoring both goals in front of 15,382 fans. And in 1978/79, the two Fourth Division encounters saw Bournemouth win 3-1 at home and draw 1-1 away. Portsmouth claimed the first double over the Cherries in the Fourth Division in 1979/80, with 1-0 and 4-0 victories at Dean Court and Fratton Park respectively, while in 1982/83, and playing one division higher, both teams won 2-0 away from home. The two Second Division clashes in 1988/89 saw Portsmouth triumph 2-1 at home and Bournemouth 1-0 at Dean Court. And the following season, in the same division, Pompey registered their second double, winning 1-0 away and 2-1 at home. In January 1991, Portsmouth recorded their biggest win over the Cherries, hammering them 5-1 in an FA Cup tie at Fratton Park in front of 15,800 spectators. Playing in League 1 in 2012/13, Bournemouth drew 1-1 away and won 2-0 at home while Portsmouth gained some revenge by winning a penalty shootout 4-3 after a 2-2 home draw in the Johnstone Paints Trophy. The last meeting between the clubs took place on Bournemouth soil in August 2013 when the Cherries won a League Cup first round game 1-0, Irish midfielder Eunan O'Kane on target in the 54th minute to the delight of the home fans in the 7,620 crowd.

SAINTS ALIVE!

Bournemouth's closest neighbours in league football are Southampton, 33.2 miles away, via the A31 and A338. So far there have been 21 competitive games played between the two clubs up to May 2015, and it's the Saints who have the better overall record with ten wins to their credit against six for the Cherries with five draws. The initial four meetings all took place in the same season, 1953/54. Saints won an FA Cup first round replay 3-1 at Dean Court in front of 13,580 fans, after a 1-1 draw at The Dell, while the two Third Division South games both resulted in home wins – 3-1 to Bournemouth and 2-1 to Saints. The two league clashes in 1954/55 both finished level, 1-1 at Dean Court and 0-0 at The Dell, before Saints completed the double in 1955/56, winning 3-2 at home and 2-1 away. In Bournemouth's excellent FA Cup season of 1956/57, they beat Saints 1-0 in their home Third Division South game, but lost 3-0 away. A total of 14 goals were scored in the two league encounters played in 1957/58. Saints won handsomely at The Dell in October, 7-0, before Bournemouth gained revenge with a worthy 5-2 home win in February. In 1958/59 the Cherries won 2-1 at home and drew 0-0 away before Southampton once again achieved their second seasonal double, winning 3-1 at Dean Court and 4-3 at the Dell in 1959/60. There was a gap of 28 years before the teams locked horns again. This time, in 1987/88, it was Bournemouth who got the better of the exchanges, winning a two-legged second round League Cup tie 3-2 on aggregate after a 2-2 away draw and a 1-0 home victory. Saints hit back by knocking the Cherries out of the same competition in 2010/11, winning their home first-round tie 2-0 with goals by future England stars Adam Lallana (a former Cherries loanee) and Alex Oxlade-Chamberlain. In the same season of League 1 football, Saints doubled up for a third time, winning 2-0 at home and 3-1 at Bournemouth when the biggest crowd of the campaign, 10,008, squeezed into Dean Court.

OFFSIDE LAW CHANGES

The first season of the present-day offside rule came into effect in 1925/26 and, in the 46 games played by Bournemouth in the Third Division South produced no less than 166 goals, 75 being scored by the Cherries. Bournemouth's first game under the new rule was against Swindon Town on 29 August 1925 and resulted in a 2-0 victory. The Cherries' biggest win of the season was 6-1 v. Crystal Palace (home) and their heaviest defeat was 8-2 in the return fixture with Swindon, while they also crashed to two 7-2 defeats, away at Bristol Rovers on Boxing Day, and Plymouth Argyle. Other big scorelines were home wins of 4-1 v. QPR, and away defeats of 5-0 at Bristol City and Charlton and 5-2 at Reading.

GOALSCORING FULL-BACK

Right-back Jack Hayward made 309 league and cup appearances for Bournemouth between 1925 and 1933, and during that time he scored a total of 33 goals, most of them penalties. Hayward also played for Bradford City and Crystal Palace.

GOALKEEPING PROBLEM

Bournemouth had a minor goalkeeping crisis early in the 2002/03 season. First-choice number one Chris Tardif was injured at Swansea on 24 August. Jamie Ashdown took over between the posts for the next two games, against Oxford United (home) on 27 August and Macclesfield Town (away) four days later. Tardif returned for the fixture at Exeter on 7 September, but was injured again and replaced by Neil Moss for the next match at home to Bury on 14 September. Later in the season the Cherries once again used three goalkeepers in quick succession – Tardif, loanee Alan Blayney and Moss. Blayney went on to win five full caps for Northern Ireland.

PENALTY REF

The Cherries have been involved in several penalty shootouts since this rule was introduced in the 1980s. There were 13 spot-kicks scored when they beat Millwall 7-6 in the shootout at the end of a 2-2 Associate Members Cup Final draw in 1983/84. The Cherries were involved in a tense penalty shootout following an extremely hard-fought Play-off semi-final against Huddersfield Town in 2010/11, but they lost 4-2. They were successful in a replayed 1991/92 FA Cup encounter with Newcastle United, winning the shootout 4-3, after 0-0 and 2-2 draws. Another FA Cup tie against Accrington Stanley in 2002/03, ended in a 5-3 defeat. After a really tough battle with near-neighbours Portsmouth in a Johnstone Paints Trophy encounter in 2012/13, the Cherries went out by losing 4-3 from the spot. A tightly-contested first round Freight Rover Trophy match against Plymouth Argyle in 1984/85 resulted in a 3-2 spot-kick victory for the Cherries, after a 2-2 draw. Following two closely fought FA Cup draws (0-0 and 2-2) with Crewe Alexandra in 2002/03, the Cherries came through 3-1 in the end-of-game shootout. And finally, against Swindon Town, also in the Freight Rover Trophy of 1986/87, the Cherries held their nerve to win the shootout 4-2 after a 0-0 draw in open play.

PENALTY SPOTS

Over a 50-year period, from August 1965 to May 2015 – and not including shootouts – Bournemouth were awarded a total of 233 penalties in competitive matches, of which 212 were successfully converted. Brett Pitman (with 20 scored) tops the Cherries' list of successful takers, followed by Ted MacDougall (11), Luther Blissett and Steve Robinson (15 each), James Hayter (ten), Rob Savage (ten), Frank Barton (seven), Lewis Grabban (seven) and Tom Heffernan (six), and Wade Elliott and Colin Russell (five each). During this same period the Cherries also conceded over 200 spot-kicks. It's swings and roundabouts, as they say. The most penalties successfully converted by a Bournemouth player in a single season is eight, by Blissett in 1990/91; Hayter struck seven in 2005/06; Grabban also fired in seven in 2013/14; Pitman bagged six in 2012/13 and five in 2009/10. Heffernan also netted five in 1982/83, as did John Sainty in 1973/74. Sheffield Wednesday's Chris Maguire equalised with a 95th-minute penalty to make it 2-2 and deny the Cherries an important victory in the home Championship game in April 2015. Bournemouth's Simon Francis had earlier been sent off.

ASSOCIATE MEMBERS CUP WINNERS

In 1983/84, Bournemouth lifted the AMC by beating Hull City 2-1 in the final at Boothferry Park. Milton Graham and Paul Morrell were the Cherries' goalscorers in front of 6,544 fans. The Cherries reached the final by beating Aldershot (4-0), Millwall (7-6 on penalties, after a 2-2 draw), Wrexham (2-0), Bristol Rovers (1-0) in the Southern Area semi-final when Robert Savage's penalty decided a tight game, and then Millwall (2-1) in the Southern Area final before a moderate crowd of 4,058 at Dean Court.

DEAN COURT FORTRESS

Bournemouth remained unbeaten at home in 1962/63. They won 11 and drew 12 of their 23 league games, scoring 39 goals and conceding only 16. They finished fifth in the Third Division on 52 points, ten adrift of champions Northampton Town.

FIRST LEAGUE DOUBLES

Bournemouth completed three doubles in their first season of league football in 1923/24. They beat Charlton Athletic 1-0 at home and 2-1 away, defeated Exeter City 1-0 at Dean Court and 2-0 at St James' Park, and edged past Queens Park Rangers 3-1 at home and 1-0 in London.

SUDDEN DEATH DEFEAT

On 19 April 1998, Bournemouth, backed by around 34,000 fans, were defeated 2-1 by Grimsby Town in the Auto Windscreens Shield Final at Wembley Stadium. The Cherries took the lead through John Bailey on 31 minutes, Jimmy Glass conceded an own goal to bring the Mariners level on 75 minutes before defender Wayne Burnett netted a sudden death winner in the 112th minute. Dave Smith (a loanee at Dean Court in 1993) and future Cherries manager Paul Groves played for Grimsby. The referee for this game came from Portsmouth – Mike Pierce. An overall crowd of 62,342 realised gate receipts of over £615,000, a record for any match involving the Cherries at that time. Bournemouth reached the final by beating Leyton Orient 2-0 in front of just 1,732 hardy supporters at Dean Court; Bristol City 1-0, also at home with 2,124 present on this occasion; Luton Town 1-0, also at home, in the Southern Area semi-final in front of 5,367 spectators and Walsall 4-3 on aggregate in the two-legged Southern Area Final. A crowd of 6,017 saw Bournemouth win 2-0 at the Bescot Stadium, Frank Rolling and Russell Beardsmore the scorers, but the Cherries then lost the return fixture 3-2, Rolling and a Wayne Evans own goal the scorers in front of an audience of 8,972, which produced club record gate receipts of £80,627.

INTO ADMINISTRATION

In February 2008, Bournemouth were forced into administration and, as a result, were docked ten points which immediately put them deep in relegation trouble at the foot of League 1. At the time the club had debts of around £4m and almost went out of business completely. The off-field uncertainty continued until the end of the season, with only one, ultimately unsuccessful, bid for the club being accepted. The Cherries, as expected at the time, were duly relegated to League 2. But they did come out of administration thanks to new owner Paul Baker and Sport-6. Prior to the start of the 2008/09 campaign, the team's future was put into doubt when the Football League threatened to block Bournemouth's participation in League 2, due to problems with the team's continuing administration worries and change in ownership. The league ordered both Bournemouth (as well as Rotherham United) to demonstrate that they could play all of their fixtures and find a way out of administration, eventually allowing the Cherries to compete with a 17-point penalty for failing to follow the League's insolvency rules. The new company was also ordered to pay unsecured creditors the amount offered at the time of the original CVA (around ten pence in the pound) within two years. Early in the season, manager Kevin Bond was sacked and was replaced by former player Jimmy Quinn, who would himself leave the club only a few months later. Another ex-player, Eddie Howe, took over as caretaker boss with the club still ten points adrift at the bottom of the League 2 table. At the time Howe was the youngest manager in the Football League at the age of 31. At the end of 2008, it was officially announced that a local businessman, Adam Murry, had completed the purchase of 50 per cent of the club's shares from previous owner/chairman Paul Baker. However, in January 2009, Murry missed the deadline to buy Baker's shares. On the final day of the 2008/09 season the Cherries guaranteed their Football League status by beating Grimsby Town 2-1, courtesy of a superb winning goal ten minutes from time by club legend Steve Fletcher. This strike sparked wild celebrations inside the ground after a fairytale ending to the 'Great Escape'. The Cherries finished their troubled season with their best away win for 30 years, thumping Morecambe 4-0 at Christie Park. In June 2009, a consortium including the aforementioned Adam Murry finally took over AFC Bournemouth. The group also included Jeff Mostyn, former vice-chairman Steve Sly, Neill Blake and one-time Dorchester Town chairman Eddie Mitchell.

HOWE'S THAT FOR PROMOTION

Eddie Howe's first full season as Bournemouth manager brought success as the Cherries finished second in League 2 to gain promotion with two games to spare.

PLAY-OFF GLORY AND DISAPPOINTMENT

In 2002/03, Bournemouth finished fourth in the Third Division to qualify for the end-of-season play-offs. In the two-legged semi-final they met Bury who they had lost both league games 2-1 to earlier in the campaign. After a battling 0-0 draw at Gigg Lane, the Cherries won their home game 3-1 before a crowd of almost 8,000. Lincoln City were the Cherries' opponents in the final at Cardiff's Millennium Stadium. In the respective league games, the Imps had won 1-0 at Dean Court while Bournemouth had earned a 2-1 victory at Sincil Bank, so a hard-fought final was anticipated. As it was, before 32,148 spectators, Bournemouth gained an excellent 5-2 win with goals from Steve Fletcher in the 29th and 77th minutes, his namesake Carl just before half-time, Stephen Purches on 56 minutes and Gareth O'Conner on the hour mark. They said that Cardiff was a City of Culture and with Bournemouth's impressive display, it was certainly that as they became the first football team to go up inside the Welsh national stadium. Eight years later, in 2010/11, unfortunately it was play-off semi-final disappointment for the Cherries when they lost on penalties to Huddersfield Town in the two-legged semi-final. The first leg on 14 May was played at Dean Court in front of 9,043 fans. It ended 1-1 with Donal McDermott equalising for the Cherries. Then, four days later before a crowd of 16,444 at the Galpharm Stadium, Bournemouth battled hard and long, and indeed, bravely, to earn a 3-3 draw after extra time for a 4-4 aggregate scoreline. But then sadly the Cherries succumbed 4-2 in the penalty shootout. Goals from Steve Lovell (two, one penalty) and Danny Ings had pushed Bournemouth into an overall 4-3 lead a minute before half-time in extra time, but Antony Kay equalised for the Terriers and this knocked the stuffing out of Lee Bradbury's team who simply couldn't respond after that. And they even missed three penalties to boot, losing the shootout 4-2. Bradbury said after the defeat, 'It was a cruel way for anyone to go out after such a great game. It is hard to take because they [the lads] really put a shift in for me. They did brilliantly and gave Huddersfield a great game. I'm immensely proud of the way they dug in. They gave me everything and that's all I can ask.'

Bournemouth's play-off record:

Venue	P	W	D	L	F	A
Home	2	1	1	0	4	2
Away	2	0	2*	0	3	3
Neutral	1	1	0	0	5	2
Totals	5	2	3	0	12	7

* Including one game lost on penalties.

HERO OFF THE BENCH

When your team has waited 42 years to reach the FA Cup third round, sometimes it takes that little extra bit of effort to make the difference – and that's what Jon Kennedy of then non-leaguers Accrington Stanley did against Bournemouth in front of the live television cameras in 2003. First-choice keeper Jamie Speare had enjoyed an impressive night, keeping the scores level at 0-0. Then, with the shootout beckoning, Stanley's manager John Coleman stunned the home crowd by replacing Speare with substitute Kennedy. The gamble paid off as Stanley went on to win the shootout 5-3, thus securing a third-round tie with Colchester. Coleman said after the game, 'I have always believed in bringing on a fresh keeper and it's the first time I have had the opportunity to do it. It was no slight on "Jamo" and I thought it might unsettle them a little bit as they would wonder what it was all about. And it did, I think.'

PROMOTION SQUAD

Bournemouth achieved the remarkable feat of gaining promotion in 2009/10 with the same 19 registered players who were at the club when relegation was suffered at the end of the previous season. In all the Cherries used just 25 players in the league, with Brett Pittman being the only ever-present.

MONEY, MONEY, MONEY

Record gate receipts of £80,267 were taken at the Bournemouth v. Walsall Auto Windscreen Shield Southern Area Final at Dean Court on 17 March 1998. This comfortably beat the club's previous record of £33,723 – taken at the turnstiles when the Cherries beat Manchester United 2-0 in a home FA Cup third round tie in January 1984. The previous best takings at a home game were £24,145 from the Third Division game with Portsmouth in February 1983. Prior to that, the club's record gate receipts were £15,466, also against Portsmouth, in a Fourth Division game in October 1979. Before that, the best was £7,326 versus Brighton & Hove Albion in the Third Division in April 1972, and £6,826 was taken at the turnstiles for the Liverpool FA Cup tie in January 1968. It is understood that from Bournemouth's home friendly with Real Madrid in 2013, the receipts amounted to around £75,000.

LOCAL CUP GAME

On 8 October 1921, a crowd of 1,500 saw Boscombe FC beat amateur team Bournemouth FC (formerly Rovers) 6-0 in an FA Cup qualifying round replay. Rovers subsequently amalgamated with another local team, the Wanderers, to become Bournemouth Poppies FC.

LAST-GAME WINNER

Darren Anderton, aged 36, scored a late winning goal for Bournemouth against Chester City on 6 December 2008. This was the former England international's 568th and final club appearance of his career (477 in the Premier League and Football League). He won 30 senior caps for his country.

FOUR GOALS IN A GAME

Six players have scored four goals in a league game for the Cherries, with one of them achieving the feat twice – Jack Russell against Clapton Orient in the Third Division South in January 1933 and against Bristol City three weeks later. The other five four-goal heroes are: Harry Mardon v. Southend United, Third Division South, January 1938; Jack McDonald v. Torquay United, Third Division South, November 1947; Ted MacDougall v. Colchester United, Third Division, September, 1970; Brian Clark v. Rotherham United, Third Division, October 1972; Luther Blissett v. Hull City, Second Division, November 1988; James Hayter v. Bury, Second Division, October 2000.

MOST LEAGUE APPEARANCES

Steve Fletcher, a Cherries legend, holds the record for most league appearances for the club – 631 made over a period spanning 15 years, between 1992 and 2007. Fletcher played 727 senior games for the Cherries, netting 121 goals, 103 in the league. Two other players who have made over 400 league appearances for the Cherries are Shaun O'Driscoll (423, 1984–95) and Ray Bumstead (412, 1958-70). Both held the club record at one time.

THE 500 CLUB

These players – who were all associated with the Cherries – amassed over 500 league appearances (north and south of the border) during their respective careers. The figures in brackets indicate the number of appearances the player made with Bournemouth:

788	David James (19)
728	Steve Fletcher (631)
693	Roger Jones (160)
641	Steve Claridge (9)
639	James Hayter (358)
626	Jimmy Case (40)
611	Brian Clark (30)
608	Gerry Peyton (202)
595	Jimmy Quinn (43)
590	David Armstrong (9)
587	Bill McGarry (78)
571	Sean O'Driscoll (423)
569	Jack Smith (42)
560	Ray Train (7)
555	David Webb (11)
554	Luther Blissett (121)
552	Matty Holland (104)
551	David Best (232)
546	Gavin Peacock (56)
543	Ian Bishop (44)
537	Kevin Bond (126)
535	Ted MacDougall (198)
530	Nigel Spackman (119)
524	Phil Boyer (141)
515	Jack Haworth (42)
514	Rio Ferdinand (10)
512	Lee Bradbury (127)
510	Mark Morris (194)
509	Frank Barton (88)

500 NOTES

Only seven players have made more league appearances than goalkeeper David James and they include Peter Shilton (1,005) and Tony Ford (931). Others who just failed to make the 500 list are John Impey (483 – 284 with Bournemouth), Darren Anderton (477), Brian Wood (476), Trevor Aylott (472), Steve Lovell (470), John Benson (468 – 150 for the Cherries),

Gary Chivers (465), Martin O'Connor (463), Steve Robinson (458) and Jack Rowley (also 458). Paul Groves, Bournemouth manager in 2012, made 669 league appearances during his career; John Bond, also boss of Bournemouth, made 511. Father and son John and Kevin Bond amassed a grand total of 1,048 League appearances between them.

LONGEST TIES

Bournemouth's longest-ever cup tie was played in 1974/75. It was against Hartlepool United in the second round of the League Cup and went to a fourth game. The initial encounter ended 1-1 at Dean Court. The replay at Victoria Park finished level at 2-2 after extra time while the second replay, again at Dean Court, also went into extra time with a final scoreline of 1-1. The third replay and fourth meeting was played at Hartlepool and resulted in a 1-0 defeat for the home side after more than 420 minutes of football (See under: League Cup Action). The Cherries have also been involved in three FA Cup ties which went to a second replay. Firstly they played Torquay United in a first round tie in 1932/33 which eventually resulted in a 3-2 second replay win for the Devon club on neutral ground at Ashton Gate. The second was against Ipswich Town, also in the first round in 1952/53, which resulted in a third-match 3-2 victory for the Tractormen at Highbury. And, in 1977/78, the Cherries took on Colchester United, again in the first round, which went in favour of the Essex club, who made progress with a 4-1 victory at Vicarage Road, Watford. The first of the Cherries' two longest League Cup ties came in 1967/68 when Watford won a first round second replay 2-1 at the County Ground, Swindon. And the second three-match game was in 1972/73, this time in the second round, when Bournemouth succumbed to Blackpool 2-1 at Villa Park. Second replays were scrapped in 1976 when the penalty shootout was introduced.

SNOW STOPS PLAY

Virtually every Football League club in the country suffered in the Arctic winters of 1947 and 1963. In 1947, the Cherries played only six Third Division South games in eight weeks, between 1 January and 28 February. They drew 0-0, 1-1 and 2-2 at Dean Court with Bristol City, Ipswich Town and Aldershot respectively, and lost 3-2 at home against Walsall, while drawing 1-1 at Brighton and losing 2-1 at Northampton. The 1946/47 season started on 31 August and finished, for some clubs, on 31 May, nine months later. The freezing cold winter of 1962/63 was far worse for many clubs. Bournemouth, in the Third Division, played only two league matches in two months, both at home, against Notts County on 22 December (won 3-1) and Northampton Town on 23 February (won

3-0). The season's league programme began on 18 August and ended on 24 May. It covered nine months and one week overall.

HONOURED

Former Bournemouth and England goalkeeper David James was awarded the MBE in the Queen's Birthday Honours List of 2012.

BIG AND SMALL CHERRIES

Irish-born forward Donal McDermott, at 6ft 6in, is one of the tallest players to appear at senior level for the Cherries, doing so in 2011/12. Goalkeeper David James, at 6ft 5in, was with the club in 2012/13, making 19 league appearances; fellow keepers Kenny Allen (1978–82) and Artur Boruc (2014/15) were both 6ft 4in, while Dutchman Franck Demouge, who was 6ft 3in in his bare feet, served the Cherries in September and October 2012. There have been scores of players measuring 6ft 2in (Miles Addison, Ryan Allsop, Jayden Stockley and Elliot Ward from recent times among them) and many as tall as 6ft 1in. Scotsman Ryan Fraser (2014/15) and Dublin-born Steve Foley-Sheridan (2006/07) are two of the smallest players to wear the colours of AFC Bournemouth, both standing 5ft 4in tall. Ian Gibson (1972/73) stood 5ft 5.5in, Sammy Igoe (1990s) 5ft 6in, 1950s winger Reg Cutler 5ft 6.5ins and Jermain Defoe (2000/01) 5ft 7in.

HEAVYWEIGHTS

Striker Trevor Aylott (1986–90), club legend Steve Fletcher and Max Thompson (1983) are among the heavyweights who have played first team football for the Cherries – all weighing around 14st in their prime.

CHRISTMAS DAY MATCHES

Bournemouth's last competitive game on a Christmas Day resulted in a 4-1 win over Reading at Dean Court in a Third Division South fixture in 1957. The game was attended by 11,162 spectators. The Cherries first played a match on 25 December 34 years earlier, in 1923, when they lost 4-2 at home to Brentford, also a Third Division South encounter, watched by a crowd of 5,032. Twenty-four hours later the Bees doubled up by winning 2-0 at Griffin Park before a crowd of 7,193. Also, on Christmas Day 1940, Bournemouth whipped visiting Bristol City 7-1 in a wartime game.

HALL FOR ONE

Between 1955 and 1968, Bournemouth had three players on their books by the name of Hall – Dennis, Peter and Richard – and only Richard, with 11 league appearances, made the first XI.

THOSE WHO GOT AWAY

All football clubs, at sometime or another, release a number of players and, after leaving, they go on to make the grade elsewhere. Among the players who left the Cherries and came good with other clubs are the following:

Player	Left club	League appearances after leaving
Adrian Ford	(0 apps, 1973)	298, Southend United, Swindon Town, Gillingham
Rod Belfitt	(trialist, 1960)	210, Leeds Utd, Ipswich, Everton, Sunderland, Fulham
Joe Birch	(26 apps, 1931)	185, all with Fulham
Walter Buckley	(0 apps, 1927)	194, Bradford PA, Lincoln City, Rochdale
Bill Cooke	(0 apps, 1938)	225, Luton Town, Shrewsbury Town, Watford
Billy Elliott	(10 apps, 1938)	170, all for West Bromwich Albion
Terrell Forbes	(3 apps, loan, 2001)	449, QPR, Grimsby Town, Oldham Athletic, Yeovil Town, Leyton Orient, Chesterfield, Aldershot
Andy Ford	(0 apps, 1973)	298, Southend United, Swindon Town, Gillingham
Steve Gritt	(6 apps, 1977)	400, Charlton Athletic, Walsall
Joe Harvey	(3 apps, 1945)	224, all for Newcastle United
Danny Ings	(27 apps. 2011)	120, all for Burnley (still playing)
Jack Johnson	(11 apps, 1930)	280, Rotherham, Barnsley, Carlisle, Accrington Stanley
Mickey Jones	(6 apps, 1928)	223, Southend United and Barrow
Barrie Meyer	(trialist, 1946)	227, Bristol Rovers, Plymouth, Newport, Bristol City
Brian Mundee	(4 apps, 1983)	116, Northampton Town, Cambridge United
Eddie Perry	(0 apps, 1930)	190, Thames, Fulham, Doncaster Rovers
Roy Proverbs	(0 apps, 1958)	143, all for Gillingham
Adrian Randall	(3 apps, 1988)	295, Aldershot, Burnley, York City, Bury

Paul Rideout ..... (0 apps, 1979) .... 413, Swindon Town, Aston Villa, Southampton, Notts County, Rangers, Everton, Tranmere Rovers

Jack Rowley .... (22 apps, 1937) .... 436, Manchester United, Plymouth Argyle

John Rutter .... (4 apps, 1973) .... 436, Exeter City, Stockport County

Eric Sibley .... (7 apps, 1938) .... 110, Blackpool, Grimsby Town, Chester

Edmund Smith . (0 apps, 1953)........... 143, Watford, Northampton Town, Colchester, QPR

Ron Smith .... (36 apps, 1961)......... 193, Crewe Alexandra, Port Vale, Southport

Jack Surtees .... (20 apps, 1933) .... 136, Northampton, Sheffield Wed, Nottingham Forest

Phil Thomas ...... (0 apps, 1972) .... 108, all for Colchester United

Bill Tunnicliffe.. (49 apps, 1933)......... 325, Wrexham, Bradford City

Ray Weigh .... (28 apps, 1951)......... 193, Stockport, Shrewsbury Town, Aldershot

Bob Young .... (1 app, 1948)............. 144, all for Crewe Alexandra

Jack Rowley scored 196 league goals after leaving Dean Court; Bill Tunnicliffe netted 53 and Danny Ings (40+ up to 2015). Winger Billy Elliott scored 157 goals in 303 games for WBA (all competitions including World War Two). Striker Paul Rideout, a 16 year-old trialist with Bournemouth, scored 109 league goals plus 23 in 99 Serie A games for Bari and one in nine SPL games for Rangers. Joe Harvey skippered Newcastle United to FA Cup Final victories in 1951 and 1952. He later managed the Geordies

THEY DIED TOO YOUNG

These are some of the many players – associated at one point with Bournemouth – who died far too young: Arnold Stephens (born 1928, died 1955, aged 27), netted 12 goals in 70 league games for the Cherries, 1948–54; Alan Groves (born in 1948, died in 1978, aged 30), scored four goals in 36 league appearances for Bournemouth between October 1972 and February 1974; Ralph Hunt (born in 1933, died in 1964, aged 31), notched 184 goals in 374 league games while assisting ten different clubs, 1950–64. He scored seven times in 33 outings for the Cherries; Phil Thomas (born 1952, died 1998, aged 46), made 108 league appearances for the Cherries, 1972–75; Alex Ritchie (born in 1904, died 1954, aged 50), a utility forward with Raith Rovers, Dunfermline Athletic, Blackpool,

Reading, Watford, Hibernian and Bournemouth, he scored 11 goals in 33 league games for the Cherries, 1933–35; George Best departed this world in 2005, aged 59 (see special feature); Dave Simmons (born in 1948, died 2007, aged 58), helped Fourth Division Colchester United knock Don Revie's Leeds United out of the FA Cup in 1971; Brynley Jones (born in 1931, died 1990, aged 59), made 118 league appearances at full-back for the Cherries, 1960–63; Dick Keith (born in 1933, died 1967, aged 44), a full-back who made 47 league appearances for the Cherries in the mid-1960s; Peter Monaghan (born in 1923, killed in action in 1944, aged 21), a left-half, he scored twice in 67 league games for the Cherries, 1937–39; Micky Reid (born in 1927, died 1975, aged 48), scored twice in five league games for the Cherries (1949/50); Micky Cave (born in 1949, died in 1985, aged 36), had two spells with the Cherries, 1971/72 and 1977, scored 20 goals for the club; Brian Tiler (born in 1943, killed in a car crash in Italy, 1990, aged 47), played for six clubs and was coach/manager of others, also Bournemouth's managing director and club secretary at the time of his death (See Harry Redknapp, managers section).

OWN GOALS

Bournemouth were gifted five own goals (four in the league) during the 1984/85 season, one helping the Cherries to a narrow 3-2 win over Derby County.

WAGES

When Bournemouth joined the Football League in 1923, the maximum wage for a senior professional was £8 a week, but by 1930 a player was averaging £1 less, picking up £7 a week. This remained the norm right up to 1945 when the maximum wage rose to £12 a week. Thereafter it went up steadily from £12 to £14, to £15, to £17, to £20 and to £25 a week by 1961. At this point the £100-a-week footballer entered the game (Johnny Haynes of Fulham) and, although specific details cannot be revealed, several players were paid 'well' by their respective clubs, and in the late 1980s/early 90s, it is known that certain players were earning £500 a week, some even more. And there is no doubt that footballers of today (2015) are on healthy contracts and quite a few are already believed to be millionaires.

ST VALENTINE'S DAY MASSACRE

On 14 February 1981, Bournemouth had a field day, thumping Bradford City 4-0 in a home Fourth Division match. A crowd of 3,561 saw London-born Dean Mooney (2), Alan Hebditch (own goal) and Trevor Morgan find the net to massacre the Bantams.

BENCH MARKERS

Billy Coxon, an outside-left and formerly of Derby County, Norwich City and Lincoln City, was the first substitute used by Bournemouth when the extra man rule was introduced for the 1965/66 season. His introduction from the bench brought his tally of league appearances for the Cherries up to a round 200. He made 309 in his career, scoring 67 goals, 37 for Bournemouth. He left Dean Court for Poole Town in July 1966 and lived in the Bournemouth area after retiring. Brett Pitman, born in St Helier, Jersey in January 1988, has made more substitute appearances than any other Bournemouth player. Up to the end of the 2014/15 season – during which he came off the bench 18 times – he had been used no less than 116 occasions as a sub by the club. He started 165 games, giving him an overall appearance total of 281 (100 goals scored). Steve Claridge (who had just one solitary outing for the Cherries) appeared in 765 club games at senior level during his career, 109 as a substitute. John O'Shea, who was on loan at Bournemouth from Manchester United in 1999/2000 (making ten league appearances), is another player who has come off the bench more than 100 times during his career for club and country. He made 89 sub appearances for the Reds alone before transferring to Sunderland in 2011. Between 1996 and 2007, striker James Hayter appeared in 407 competitive games for Bournemouth, scoring 108 goals. He had 358 outings in the league (94 goals) and was called off the bench 63 times as a Cherry. After leaving the club, he continued to perform well and in 2014 reached the personal milestone of 600 league appearances when playing for Yeovil Town, over 100 of which came as a second-half substitute. He had made 723 club appearances (152 as a substitute) and notched 176 goals at the end of the 2014/15 season. Cherries legend Steve Fletcher made 727 first-class appearances for the Cherries (591 starts, 136 as a substitute). His career in league and cup football realised a grand total of 834 club appearances, of which 191 came as a sub. His league stats alone were 556 games played plus 172 as a substitute. Josh McQuoid made 23 substitute appearances for the Cherries in one single season, 2009/10. Alan Connell made 19 and Steve Fletcher 17 in the same campaign. In fact, 47 of McQuoid's first 65 senior appearances for the Cherries were made as a substitute. Danish striker Claus Jorgensen made a total of 349 league appearances during his career (1999–2009), of which 89 came as a substitute. Similarly, Tresor Kandol played in almost 200 league games (1998–2009) with 68 coming as a sub. Scottish U21 international Robert Murray, who was born in Hammersmith, London, made 147 league appearances for Bournemouth between September 1992 and May 1998 – 59 as a substitute. He actually started 100 senior games for the club, played in 174 overall, 74 as a sub. Quite versatile, he could occupy a defensive or attacking position. He holds the record of being the youngest league debutant for Wolves in 1992. Dani (the Portuguese Under-21 international) made 62 sub appearances during his two spells with the club (1998/99 and 2004/05). Jason Tindall made 50 appearances as a sub for the Cherries during his first spell at the club, 1998–2008. Wade Elliott made over 250 appearances for the Cherries (2000–05), 45 as a sub. Gareth O'Connor, a Dublin-born midfielder, spent five years with the Cherries (2000–05) during which time he played in 204 games, 66 as a substitute. During his professional career, Irish international Warren Feeney made 325 league appearances of which 115 came as a substitute. He had 93 games for the Cherries (2001–04), 32 as a sub. Scotsman Derek Holmes, born in Lanark and formerly of Hearts and Ross County, played for Bournemouth from September 2001 until February 2005. During that time he made 136 first-class appearances, 64 as a substitute (52 in the league). Alan O'Connell started 22 games for the Cherries and came on in another 42, making it 64 appearances in total. Born in Enfield, he served the club for three years from 2002–05. Marcus Browning was another well-used substitute. He was a Cherry from 2002 until 2007, during which time he made 214 first-team appearances, 37 as a sub. Adam Smith (23), Brett Pitman (18), Dan Gosling (17), Yann Kermorgant (12) and Adam Fraser (12) made the most sub appearances for the Cherries in 2014/15.

HOT AND COLD PLAY

On 28 August 1926, when Bournemouth played Aberdare Athletic in a Third Division South game in South Wales, the recorded temperature at pitch level during the game was 82 fahrenheit (27.7 celsius). This is said to be one of the hottest days ever recorded on a day when the Cherries when in action. In stark contrast, when Bournemouth played Luton Town at Dean Court in a league game on 8 February 1969, the on-field temperature was said to have dropped to four degrees below freezing.

YOUNG PLAYERS

Jimmy White was just 15 years and 321 days old when he made his senior debut for the Cherries – in a Third Division South game against Brentford on 30 April 1958. Defender Rob Murray was 17 years and 391 days old when he made his Football League debut for the Cherries at Blackpool in September 1992. Future Bournemouth forward Cameron Buchanan, a Scot from Holytown near Airdrie, was only 14 years and 57 days old when he played for Wolverhampton Wanderers against West Bromwich Albion in a Wartime League North game in September 1942. He joined the Cherries in 1949.

RECORD SALES AND SIGNINGS

When striker Danny Ings was sold to Burnley in August 2011, Bournemouth received a club-record incoming fee of £1m. And when the Cherries signed Tyrone Mings from Ipswich Town in June 2015, the £8m was a record outlay by the Cherries, although Ryan Fraser did switch to Portman Road as part of the deal. Brett Pitman also left the Cherries for the Suffolk club in a separate deal. Other big-money (and record) signings made by the Cherries:

£2.5m ....for Tokelo Rantie from FF Malmo (Sweden), August 2013
£840,000........for Matt Tubbs from Crawley Town, January 2012
£250,000........for Steve Lovell from Portsmouth, August 1999
£210,000........for Gavin Peacock from Gillingham, August 1989
£110,000........for Bobby Barnes from Swindon Town, March 1989
£90,000 ....for Shaun Close from Tottenham Hotspur, February 1988
£70,000 ....for Brian Clark from Cardiff City, October 1972
£31,000 ....for Harry Redknapp from West Ham United, June 1972
£20,000 ....for Phil Boyer from York City, December 1970
£10,000 ....for Ted MacDougall from York City, July 1969
£10,000 ....for Keith Miller from West Ham United, July 1970

Other record outgoing transfers by the Cherries:
£880,000........Matt Holland to Ipswich Town, July 1997
£800,000........Joe Parkinson to Everton, March 1994
£765,000 ....Efan Ekoku to Norwich City, March 1993
£465,000 ....Ian Bishop to Manchester City, August 1989
£350,000.........Colin Clarke to Southampton, June 1986
£195,000 ....Ted MacDougall to Manchester United, September 1972
£30,000 ....Roger Jones to Blackburn Rovers, January 1970

RECORD LEAGUE SEQUENCES

Longest run of wins: eight from 12 March 2013 to 20 April 2013
Longest run of defeats: seven from 13 August 1994 to 13 September 1994
Longest run of draws: five from 25 April 2000 to 12 August 2000
Longest unbeaten run: 18 games, from 6 March 1982 to 28 August 1982
Longest winless run: 14 games from 6 March 1974 to 27 April 1974
Successive scoring run: 31 games from 28 October 2000 to 5 May 2001
Longest non-scoring run: six games from 1 February 1975 to 13 March 1975
Bournemouth have lost seven home League games in a row on two occasions – between 1 November 1952 and 27 December 1952, and 14 September 1955 and 8 October 1955.

The Cherries lost 12 successive away league games over a period of eight

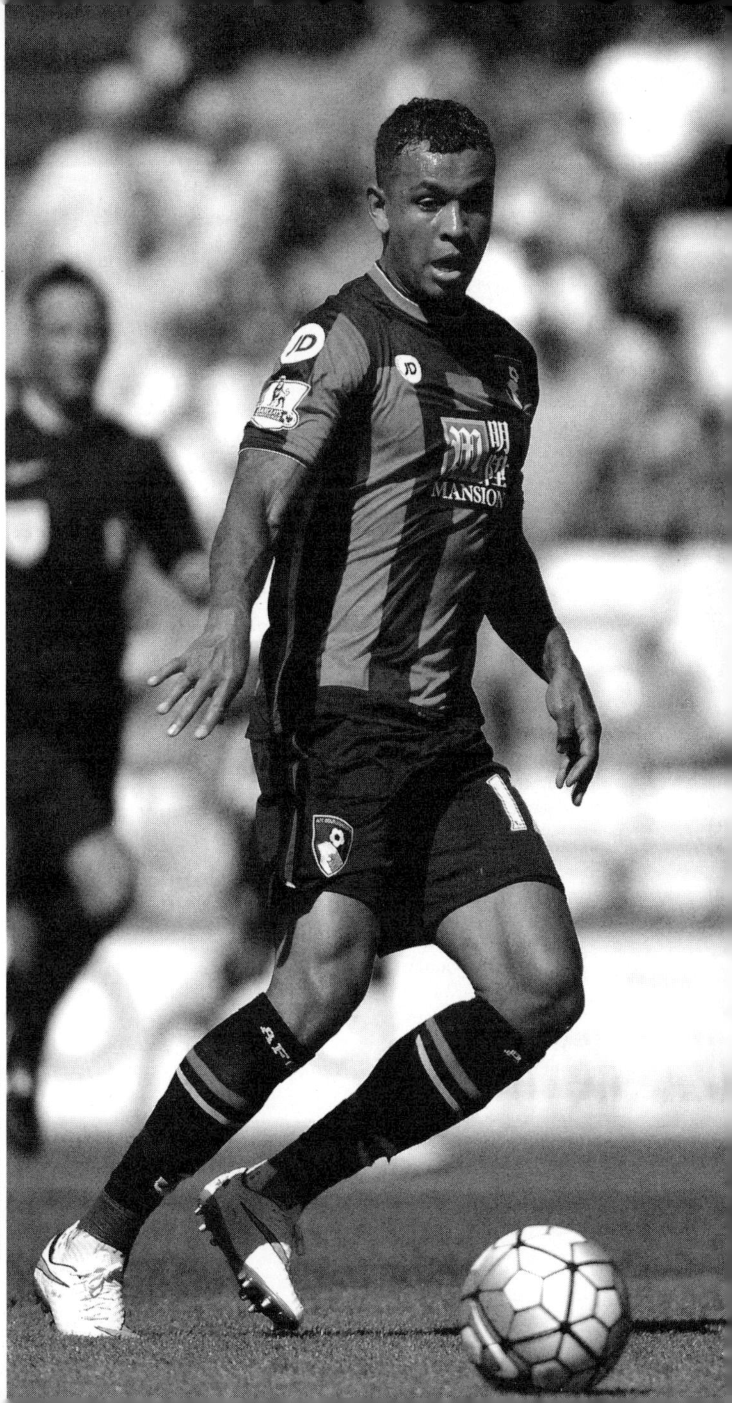

RECORD SIGNING TYRONE MINGS

months, between Boxing Day 1933 and 27 August 1934.

Between 7 April 1962 and 19 October 1963, Bournemouth went 33 home league games without defeat. Fourteen of these matches ended in draws.

The Cherries' 31-match scoring run finally came to an end when they lost 1-0 to Huddersfield Town on the opening day of the 2001/02 season.

The last win of that eight-in-a-row sequence in March and April 2013 was 3-1 at home to Carlisle United. The run ended with a 0-0 draw at Tranmere on the last day of the season. And it was a result that cost the Cherries the title. Victory at Prenton Park would have taken them a point clear of Doncaster Rovers, who were champions with 84 points to Bournemouth's 83. The eight wins came against Stevenage 1-0, Oldham Athletic 1-0, Bury 4-1, Colchester United 1-0, Scunthorpe United 1-0, Notts County 3-1, Shrewsbury Town 3-1, and Carlisle.

DRAW SPECIALISTS – AGAIN

In 2005/06, Bournemouth equalled a club record (set in 1981/82) by drawing 19 of their 46 League 1 games. Eleven came at home, eight away.

GOAL FAMINE

An alarming goal famine struck Bournemouth in 1968/69 when they scored only 19 times in their last 22 league matches. They failed to find the net in ten of those games and the agonising run cost them promotion as they finished fourth in the Third Division. Seven years later, the Cherries managed to score only two goals in 12 league games between 1 February and 29 March 1975.

TEN-GOAL CLASH

In January 1975, Plymouth Argyle (third) visited Bournemouth (20th) for a Third Division encounter which, taking into consideration the respective positions of the two teams, was vitally important. At half-time the visitors led 4-0 and went on to win the game 7-3, inflicting upon Bournemouth one of their worst home defeats. A crowd of 7,352 saw future Cherry Billy Rafferty score for the Pilgrims.

STAYING PUT

Bournemouth played Third Division football from 1923 until 1970 – a record. They were relegated to the fourth sector at the end of the 1969/70 season, but regained their status at the first attempt.

RUN BROKEN

On the 25 November 1995, Bournemouth's excellent run of not conceding a league goal for 699 minutes came to an end at Chesterfield when Phil Robinson found the net for the Spireites in a 3-0 win at Saltergate.

LATE FLOURISH BY EYRE

On 5 March 1927, with barely 20 minutes remaining of the Third Division South game between Merthyr Town and Bournemouth in South Wales, the teams stood level at 4-4, Jack Phillips having scored all of Merthyr's goals. But Ronnie Eyre netted a hat-trick for the Cherries, who went on to win 6-4.

GOLDEN GOAL

In May 1946, Bournemouth met Queens Park Rangers in the replay of the Third Division South Cup semi-final. At the end of 90 minutes the game stood goalless and remained so after three periods of extra time. So it was agreed that the match should continue and whoever scored next would win, and the referee end the contest. As it was, Jack Kirkham did the trick for the Cherries, hitting the back of the QPR net in the 136th minute. This is also the longest game involving Bournemouth.

PACK OF WOLVES

Over a ten-year period, 1930–39 inclusive, no less than 38 former or future Wolverhampton Wanderers players were registered with Bournemouth at various levels. They were: Len Adkins, Walter Akers, George Bellis, Kenny Bird, John Bradford, Ted Buckley, Wilf Bucknall, Meynell Burgin, Roy Burns, Bill Colley, Billy Elliott, George Farrow, Jack Flaherty, Billy Gold, Joe Harvey, Arthur Keeley, Reg Kirkham, Billy Langley, George Lax, James Lovery, John McDonald, Fred Marsden, Ronnie Morgan, Tom Paton, Fred Pincott, Robert Redfern, Jack Rowley (loan), Billy Sellars, Len Smart, George Smith, Billy Smith, Ernie Tagg, Eden Taylor, John Turner, Richard Twiss, Ernie Whittam, Fred Wilson and Laurie Woodward. Other players who, over the years, have donned the old gold strip and also starred for the Cherries, include Vince Bartram, Cameron Buchanan, Ken Charlton, Steve Claridge, Fred Davies, Ken Holland (amateur), George Marshall, Neil Masters, Graham Newton, Tom Paton, Billy Rafferty, Micky Reid, John Rutter, Arnold Stephens, Sam Vokes and Gareth Williams. And of course there is Bill McGarry, who managed both clubs.

TOUGH GOING

Outside-left Billy Hutchinson started playing football in 1926. He joined Bournemouth in 1930 but left Dean Court within a year, teaming up with Leeds United. After leaving Elland Road, he assisted Darlington and Halifax Town before retiring in 1933, having made only seven league appearances in seven years, two for the Cherries.

NINE-GOAL THRILLER

In August 1989, Bournemouth looked comfortable at half-time in their league game with Hull City. They were leading 4-1 and the visitors were struggling to keep the eager Cherries forwards at bay. But after the break it was a different story. The Tigers began to roar and they made a contest of it before Paul Moulden completed his hat-trick to give the Cherries a narrow 5-4 victory. Later in the season Bournemouth completed the double over Hull with an excellent 4-1 win on Humberside. A year earlier, in November 1988, Luther Blissett scored four times when the Cherries beat the Tigers 5-1 at Dean Court after a goalless first-half.

DISASTROUS START

Bournemouth lost their first seven league games at the start of the 1994/95 season (a club record) and suffered 12 defeats in their opening 14 fixtures. Finding themselves rock bottom of the table, they improved greatly during the second half of the campaign and eventually edged themselves to safety, finishing in 19th position and avoiding relegation by just two points (see below).

THE GREAT ESCAPE

With two games left to play at the end of the 1994/95 season, Bournemouth (44 points), Cambridge United (44) and Plymouth Argyle (42) were all in danger of being relegated to the Third Division along with Cardiff City and Leyton Orient. Bournemouth also had a better goal difference than Cambridge, but not Plymouth. It turned out to be a very tense and nailbiting finale. Bournemouth needed to win both of their matches, away at Brentford and at home to Shrewsbury Town, to stand any chance of surviving the trap door. Plymouth had to visit Wycombe and play Oxford United at home, while Cambridge had a home fixture with Huddersfield and an away trip to Wrexham. The first round of matches ended in wins for both Bournemouth and Plymouth while Cambridge drew, meaning that the points totals, with one game remaining, were Bournemouth 47, Cambridge 45 and Plymouth 45. It was simple mathematics – the Cherries

HAD to beat the Shrews to stay up, and they did just that, winning 3-0 in front of Dean Court's biggest crowd of the season, 10,757, and the best on the ground since February 1989 when 11,571 attended the league game with West Bromwich Albion. First-half goals from Steve Robinson (2) and Scott Mean did the trick as the Cherries pulled off what was surely the classic Great Escape on the Dorset Coast. It was a great achievement by manager Mel Machin and his merry men – a wonderful end-of-season performance, but why did they leave it so late?

BOURNEMOUTH LADIES

Bournemouth Ladies football club was formed in 1999 and originally had two teams – Charlie's Angels and Dorset Devils. After making steady progress, the club joined the Dorset Women's League (open-age) and entered the Dorset Cup in 2002/03, and although they lost their first game 7-2 against Corfe Hills, the ladies battled on gamely, won a few matches and attracted several new players, mainly from Bournemouth University and Southampton Saints. With a stronger squad, the female Cherries went on to win the cup (beating Dorchester Town in the final) and also finished runners-up in the league to clinch promotion in their first season, which ended with a 16-3 revenge victory over Corfe Hills. Over the last 12 years or so, the ladies have continued to perform well in various league and cup competitions, and are now setting their sights on reaching the FA Women's Premier League. 'If the men can do it, so can we,' said one confident young lass.

THE STORY OF THE 'OTHER' BOURNEMOUTH FOOTBALL CLUB

The club was founded on 11 September 1875 at a meeting held inside Abbotts Auction Mart on Old Christchurch Road which was attended by eight football enthusiasts, presided over by Alderman J. Nethercoate, who later became the Lord Mayor of Bournemouth. Initially it was decided to name the club Bournemouth Rovers and to this day, it is regarded as being one of the oldest football clubs in the country. Founder members of the Football Association, then the Hampshire FA and also the Bournemouth FA, the team (wearing all white) then played as Bournemouth Dean Park, before settling on the name of Bournemouth FC which was adopted in 1889, having amalgamated with another local side, Bournemouth Arabs. Up to joining the Wessex League in 1986, Bournemouth FC had played entirely in the Hampshire League, except for a short spell at the turn of the 20th century. Earliest records show that the team played an FA Cup tie in November 1884 and were beaten 6-0 in a first round encounter by

Old Westminsters at Kennington Oval, home of Surrey CCC and, over the next two seasons, were eliminated early on by Old Etonians (twice winners of the trophy in 1879 and 1882) and Chatham. In their first season in the Hampshire League, 1896/97, Bournemouth finished sixth (of eight) and over the next few years, the team played on three different pitches – on East Common near the Bournemouth railway station, on Dean Park (the current home of Dorset County Cricket) and at Victoria Park, formerly a farmer's field. The first taste of county success came in 1904/05 when Bournemouth won the West Division, and they repeated this feat in 1909/10. Nicknamed the Poppies, Bournemouth then lifted the County Division championship in 1913/14 and 1921/22, and won the Hampshire League Shield in 1912/13, with Jack Wheeler scoring 76 goals in 47 matches during that season. His haul included nine strikes in a 19-day period. Progress was made in the FA Amateur Cup in 1923/24, when Bournemouth reached the third round only to lose 1-0 at home against Botwell Mission, who in later years changed their name to Hayes. Unfortunately, at the end of the 1928/29 season, Bournemouth slipped into the newly formed Division Two, but bounced back quickly, regaining top flight status as champions in 1931/32. However the club languished in the bottom half of Division One for several seasons before finally falling back into Division Two when football resumed after the World War Two. To their credit the club recovered again and won the Hampshire Intermediate Cup in 1949/50, but then had to wait 20 years before lifting more silverware, winning the Intermediate Cup for a third time in 1971/72. After regaining Division One status in 1978/79, Bournemouth were relegated again in 1980/81, but agonisingly they fell into Division Three in 1982/83 before switching to the newly-formed Wessex League for the 1985/86 season. Bournemouth FC, despite some bold attempts, have yet to win the Wessex League. They finished third in 1990/91 and runners-up in 1994/95, edged out by Fleet Town. The first trophy – for a number of years – finally arrived at the club in 2010/11 when Bournemouth won the League Cup, beating Winchester City 1-0 in the final. The following season the Poppies reached the FA Carlsberg Vase quarter-final for the very first time, but were knocked out at this crucial stage 2-0 at home by West Auckland Town. The 2012/13 season is best forgotten. The horrible weather throughout the campaign didn't help one iota – bad pitches, abandonments, injured players, being the major problems. But things improved, slowly, and Bournemouth are now hoping to press hard for honours in the next few years.

ROVERS FACTFILE

The first official game played by Bournemouth Rovers at the club's Dean Park ground was on 12 February 1876. A crowd of 200 saw the visitors, the Panthers from Blandford, win 1-0. In the return fixture, played a week later at Baileygate, the Panthers romped home 4-0.

• On Tuesday evening, 26 November 1878, Bournemouth played a game under experimental electric lights at Dean Park for 'a grand exhibition of the new electric light'. Conditions in general weren't perfect and part of a cinder cycle track was cut into the field of play.

• The club has also changed name from Bournemouth Rovers, to Bournemouth Wanderers and now Bournemouth Poppies.

• Bournemouth FC changed the colour of their shirts several times before adopting the colour poppy red in 1895/96 – switching from green and white hoops following the merger with Bournemouth Wanderers.

• One of the club's most famous members is William Pickford, who later became chairman of the Football Association. Also, along with Alfred Gibson, he wrote *Association Football and the Men Who Made It* – the history of the game from 1872, produced in four volumes in 1905/06.

• Another is Joseph Joy, a local landowner and supporter, who gave the present Namu Road ground to the club.

• The club's present ground – Victoria Park – is situated in the middle of several houses and remains much as it was when they first moved there in 1908. Bournemouth Council bought the ground outright in October 1944 for £3,750, providing a lease on a peppercorn rent.

• In April 1911 – following a request via friends of the club who were living in Dortmund – Bournemouth went on a short tour to Germany. A party of 16 travelled, including the team manager and trainer, and these players: Marsh, Burry, Belbin, Hayter, Lane, Smith, Beaumont, Gill, Griffith, Mellor and Lawson. Three friendly matches were played; two were won (5-1 v. Hilden and 3-2 v. Dortmund) and one drawn (3-3 with Duisburg).

• The clubhouse and changing rooms were officially opened in 1985, and the current 205-seater stand provides adequate cover from the elements with several rows of bench seating replacing the old wooden stand which was destroyed by fire. This stretches about a third of the length of the pitch – next to the glass-fronted clubhouse. The remaining three sides are simple flat terracing, separated from the playing area by a metal barrier.

AND FINALLY

In the summer of 1965, the players of AFC Bournemouth were in pre-season training before embarking on another programme of Third Division matches against the likes of Exeter City, Grimsby Town, Mansfield

Town, Oxford United, Scunthorpe United, Workington and York City. How times have changed. Fifty years later Eddie Howe and his squad spent their summer planning to take on Chelsea, Arsenal, Manchester City, Manchester United and Tottenham, play in front of 75,000 fans at Old Trafford and 60,000 at The Emirates, as well as featuring every weekend on *Match of the Day*.

CLUB DETAILS 2015

Address: AFC Bournemouth, Vitality Stadium, Dean Court, Kings Park, Bournemouth, Dorset BH7 7AF
Telephone number: (0844) 576 1910
Fax number: (0121) 726 373
E-mail: enquiries@afcb.co.uk
Commercial Department: commercial@afcb.co.uk
Club Store: clubshop@afcb.co.uk
Ticket Office: tickets@afcb.co.uk
Bournemouth Ladies FC: afcbl.cjb.net www./afcbladies.co.uk

CLUB PERSONNEL

Chairman: Jeff Mostyn
Chief executive: Neill Blake
Club owner: Maxim Demin
Head of media/communications: Max Fitzgerald
Team manager: Eddie Howe
Assistant manager: Jason Tindall
First team coach: Simon Weatherstone
Development squad manager: Stephen Purches
Physiotherapist: Steve Hard
Head of sports science: Dan Hodges
Performance analyst: Garvan Stewart
Sports therapist: Dave Gardener
Kit manager: Chris Jeffes
Club ambassador: Steve Fletcher